James Joyce

THE PROFILES IN LITERATURE SERIES

GENERAL EDITOR: B. C. SOUTHAM, M.A., B.LITT. (OXON.)
*Formerly Department of English, Westfield College,
University of London*

Volumes in the series include

James Joyce

by Arnold Goldman
Lecturer in English and American Studies
University of Sussex

LONDON

ROUTLEDGE & KEGAN PAUL

NEW YORK: HUMANITIES PRESS

First published 1968
by Routledge and Kegan Paul Ltd
Broadway House, 68–74 Carter Lane
London, E.C.4

Printed in Great Britain
by Northumberland Press Limited
Gateshead

SBN 7100 2951 9

The Profiles in Literature Series

This series is designed to provide the student of literature and the general reader with a brief and helpful introduction to the major novelists and prose writers in English, American and foreign literature.

Each volume will provide an account of an individual author's writing career and works, through a series of carefully chosen extracts illustrating the major aspects of the author's art. These extracts are accompanied by commentary and analysis, drawing attention to particular features of the style and treatment. There is no pretence, of course, that the study of extracts can give a sense of the works as a whole, but this selective approach enables the reader to focus his attention upon specific features, and to be informed in his approach by experienced critics and scholars who are contributing to the series.

The volumes will provide a particularly helpful and practical form of introduction to writers whose works are extensive or which present special problems for the modern reader, who can then proceed with a sense of his bearings and an informed eye for the writer's art.

An important feature of these books is the extensive reference list of the author's works and the descriptive list of the most useful biographies, commentaries and critical studies.

In this volume Dr. Goldman draws attention to the special relationship between Joyce's life and his writing. The passages are presented in chronological order, with a commentary which pays due attention to the biographical aspects of Joyce's art.

B.C.S.

Contents

CONTENTS

'FINNEGANS WAKE'

CONTENTS

Acknowledgments

The author and publisher wish to thank the following for permission to use copyright material:

The Bodley Head Ltd., for extracts from *Ulysses*; Jonathan Cape Ltd. and the Executors of the James Joyce Estate, for extracts from *Dubliners* and *A Portrait of the Artist as a Young Man*; The Society of Authors, as the literary representative of the Estate of the late James Joyce, for extracts from *Finnegans Wake*.

A note on the pagination of extracts

As Joyce did not number the chapters of *Ulysses* and *Finnegans Wake* and divided *A Portrait of the Artist as a Young Man* into only five untitled chapters, it has been thought best to give *page* references for the extracts in *The Profile Joyce*. The current British editions to which these page references relate are:

for *Dubliners* and *A Portrait of the Artist as a Young Man*, *The Essential James Joyce*, ed. Harry Levin (Penguin Books, 1963);
for *Ulysses*, the Bodley Head edition of 1960;
for *Finnegans Wake*, the Faber & Faber edition of 1939, as corrected in 1964.

The texts used for the extracts have been corrected by the present editor to conform with scholarly standards.

Biographical note

James Joyce was born on February 2, 1882, in a suburb of Dublin, Ireland. Through a series of financial reverses and inability to hold a job, his father John Joyce gradually impoverished himself and his family. Through his father's connexions, and later by his own abilities, Joyce won a series of scholarships to two of the best Catholic schools in Ireland, Clongowes Wood and Belvedere Colleges. He was an exceptional young scholar and won a number of prizes for English in national Irish academic competitions.

After a period during which he considered taking orders in the Roman Catholic Church, Joyce decided instead on a secular life. He graduated B.A. from Dublin's then Catholic Royal University, in 1902, where he specialised in English, French and Italian. His marks were erratic, high only in what took his present interest. He was an excellent linguist and for a time supported himself, and later his wife and children, by teaching in language schools on the Continent.

Before he left Ireland in 1904, Joyce had composed a collection of thirty-six poems, *Chamber Music*, had written a number of chapters of an 'autobiographical' novel, and most of the short stories published collectively as

Dubliners in 1914. In 1916, the final version of his first novel was published, titled *A Portrait of the Artist as a Young Man*, and Joyce was already at work on his long comic epic *Ulysses*, whose chapters appeared in periodicals as he wrote them and were printed together in 1922. From 1922 to 1939, at times incapacitated by a severe eye-disease, Joyce laboured at *Finnegans Wake*, a second comic epic, his 'summa' or consciously undertaken master-work which, like certain other epics, was to engage its author for the rest of his writing life.

Introduction to the novels

Born in Dublin, Joyce lived on the Continent from 1904, notably in Trieste, Zurich and Paris, and died in 1941, at the age of fifty-eight, in Zurich. This 'European' life is an apt reflection of his place in the international artistic movement of the early twentieth century, a movement which encouraged a supra-national 'European' idea of the arts. Many of the artists and writers involved were as interested in the 'aesthetic' as the social aspect of culture, and the leading professors, Joyce included, have a reputation for artistic *experimentation* of a superficially tradition-shattering nature.

Literary experimenters can be of the slapdash or of the painstaking kinds: Joyce was the latter. He laboured with craftsmanlike precision over each of his works. Unlike the Victorian novelist Trollope, who also wrote in a workmanlike manner, Joyce did not turn out his novels at regular intervals. He took ten years to write *A Portrait of the Artist as a Young Man*, seven to write *Ulysses* and seventeen for *Finnegans Wake*.

From the beginning Joyce found himself at the centre of those controversies which have been a characteristic feature of experimental or *avant-garde* art in this century. First his writing was thought too realistic, too detailed and even sordid in its depiction of ordinary and 'low' life. Objections on this score kept *Dubliners* from being published for a number of years after its completion in 1906.

Eventually Joyce was to become controversial not only for his realism but also for a kind of writing which is realism's polar opposite and which goes under the names of formalism, symbolism, impressionism and modernism. Their common denominator is a decided emphasis on techniques of presentation, as distinct from subject-matter. The charge which the unsympathetic or uncomprehending levy against the formalism of Joyce—or Picasso in art, or Schoenberg in music—is that their work is of the head rather than the heart, is too difficult, artificial and cerebral for most readers either to understand or enjoy. Supporters deny the charge of heartlessness and claim that only such difficult art can engage their full attention as both feeling and thinking people.

James Joyce straddled both major movements of modern literature, realism and symbolism. Their combination is undoubtedly a particularly characteristic feature of his writings.

Even in *Dubliners*, the commonness, even sordidness of setting and action, is enfolded in a highly mannered prose style. Here, from the very first story in the collection, 'The Sisters', the narrator describes his visit as a boy to 'the house of mourning' wherein lies coffined a dead priest he had known.

I

In the evening my aunt took me with her to visit the house of mourning. It was after sunset; but the windowpanes of the houses that looked to the west reflected the tawny gold of a great bank of clouds. Nannie received us in the hall; and, as it would have been unseemly to have shouted at her, my aunt shook hands with her for all. The old woman pointed upwards interrogatively and, on my aunt's nodding, proceeded to toil up the narrow staircase before us, her bowed head being scarcely above the level of the banister-rail. At the first landing she stopped and beckoned us forward encouragingly towards the open door of the dead-room. My aunt went in and the old woman, seeing that I hesitated to enter, began to beckon to me again repeatedly with her hand.

I went in on tiptoe. The room through the lace end of the blind was suffused with dusky golden light amid which the candles looked like pale thin flames. He had been coffined. Nannie gave the lead and we three knelt down at the foot of the bed. I pretended to pray but I could not gather my thoughts because the old woman's mutterings distracted me. I noticed how clumsily her skirt was hooked at the back and how the heels of her cloth boots were trodden down all to one side.

Dubliners, p. 358

The clumsily hooked skirt and the trodden-down *cloth* boots point in the direction of realism, but the experience also includes 'the tawny gold' of the clouds and the 'dusky golden light' in the room. The almost romantic formality in not only in the words; it is in the rhythms as well. Note how the sentences which include these phrases flow on well past where they might end. The prose is heavily cadenced.

Now that we have a fuller knowledge of Joyce's own life, we can see—from his letters and reported conversation—what this shaping and mannering of his prose meant to him. In part it may have been a form of condescension, a way of asserting that he was finer (more

3

subtle, discriminating and sophisticated) than the squalid Dubliners about whom he wrote.

Equally important was the necessity he felt to wrestle this ordinary and crude material into 'beauty' by a form of expression which would satisfy his aesthetic sensibility. At times he saw these two dimensions as antithetical, contradictory: as a young man he wrote essays about the conflict of the 'realistic' (or 'classic') and the 'romantic' (or 'symbolic') in art.

The young Joyce's divided loyalties are apparent in his earliest collection, *Epiphanies*. These are very short prose pieces—only published after Joyce's death—named after the discovery of the Christ child by the Magi, in the Roman Catholic year the Feast of the Epiphany. The word means a 'showing forth' of reality. Some of Joyce's 'epiphanies' appear designed to catch characters unconsciously exposing themselves, while others are obvious attempts of the writer to compose a prose poem, usually via natural description. In the following passage, the protagonist of *A Portrait of the Artist* 'thinks' one of these epiphanies, musing about a man said to be descended from 'an incestuous love':

2

The park trees were heavy with rain and rain fell still and ever in the lake, lying grey like a shield. A game of swans flew there and the water and the shore beneath were fouled with their green-white slime. They embraced softly, impelled by the grey rainy light, the wet silent trees, the shieldlike witnessing lake, the swans. They embraced without joy or passion, his arm about his sister's neck. A grey woollen cloak was wrapped athwart her from her shoulder to her waist: and her fair head was bent in willing shame. He had loose redbrown hair and tender shapely strong freckled hands. Face. There was no face seen. The brother's face was bent upon her fair rainfragrant hair. The hand freckled and strong and shapely and caressing was Davin's hand.

A Portrait of the Artist, p. 232

In its context in the novel, this epiphany becomes less straightforward. There its romanticising appears as part of the personality of the character who thinks it. A moment later the character 'frown[s] angrily upon his thought', noticing that with the inclusion of 'Davin' (another character) he has drifted off into dream-fantasy, into his subconscious, and away from proper artistic creation.

Joyce was a natural mimic, and in a manner of speaking his works exploit mimicry more and more progressively. In *Dubliners* he often phrases things when speaking as the narrator in words the characters might have used.

In *A Portrait of the Artist*, mimicry was extended even further. When Stephen Dedalus, the main character, is an infant, the novel is written for a few pages in baby-talk:

He was baby tuckoo. The moocow came down the road where Betty Byrne lived: she sold lemon platt.

O, the wild rose blossoms
On the little green place.

He sang that song. That was his song.

O, the green wothe botheth.

A Portrait of the Artist, p. 53

When Stephen is a schoolboy Joyce allows his own prose to approximate a schoolboy's: not entirely, but Joyce's prose covers a spectrum, with his personal comment at one end and Stephen and his boy-contemporaries' speech at the other; in between is a mixed middle-ground, part Joyce, part Stephen.

So the novel proceeds, altering its style to suit the age of the main character. Mimicry carried this far is sometimes called 'imitative form'.

Joyce's interest in miming the speech-styles of his characters passes over into an interest in their thought-styles as well and his reproduction of the course of a character's thought is the feature of his mature writing for which he is undoubtedly most well-known. The technique which he developed for this purpose is usually called the 'stream of consciousness'. In the following example from *Ulysses* we can see how the character thinks in staccato bursts, but omits to 'punctuate' his thought when he 'remembers' a relevant fact.

3

Nice soft tweed Ned Lambert has in that suit. Tinge of purple. I had one like that when we lived in Lombard street west. Dressy fellow he was once. Used to change three suits in the day. Must get that grey suit of mine turned by Mesias. Hello. It's dyed. His wife I forgot he's not married or his landlady ought to have picked out those threads for him.

Ulysses, p. 139

The paragraph is a little drama. Alas, Ned Lambert has fallen from his former heights of sartorial splendour!

These 'streams of consciousness', while making up a large portion of *Ulysses*, are by no means the whole of the novel, nor are they its only literary innovation.

For one thing, the whole present action of this very long novel takes place in some eighteen hours. *Ulysses* has a dedication to detail hardly matched in world literature: it has *more* plot in its one day than writers previously thought to include as relevant to action. Further, the novel follows, in a generally alternating way, two characters on their daily round in Dublin. One is the same Stephen Dedalus of *A Portrait of the Artist*, now two years older, thinking of quitting his lodgings, leaving his job as a schoolteacher and perhaps abandoning Ireland for good. (His first trip abroad, to Paris, had lasted only a few months.) The other principal character is an advertising canvasser named Leopold Bloom. During the day Bloom pursues his job in a desultory sort of way, but mainly his mind is on his domestic situation, for he has discovered that his wife has arranged an assignation with another man for that very afternoon.

Among the ways by which Joyce organised his novel about these two 'wandering' characters, Dedalus and Bloom (who finally meet during the evening), is one startling method, signified by the book's title, *Ulysses*—the Roman name for the Greek hero of Homer's *Odyssey*. In Joyce's novel, Leopold Bloom becomes a kind of Odysseus (or Ulysses), who spent ten years attempting to return home after the Trojan War.

The primary relationship between *Ulysses* and the *Odyssey* is apparently ironical: Bloom's wife, Molly, unlike Ulysses' Penelope, is not faithfully awaiting his arrival, holding her suitors at bay; Stephen Dedalus, the Telemachus of the novel (Ulysses' son), is searching for a 'father' (having abandoned his real father, his Church and his state) and discovers not a great hero, but only the cuckolded Bloom. But behind this irony there may be some sympathy: perhaps Bloom is a kind of hero after all, perhaps Stephen sees this.

Joyce makes a number of events in *Ulysses* parallel those in Homer's epic. He thought of each chapter as having a parallel episode in the *Odyssey*, although he did not publish his Homeric chapter-titles when *Ulysses* was printed. Some of the fun of reading Joyce's comic novel can come from recognising Joyce's Homeric allusions and their attendant ironies. For example, Odysseus uses a sharpened stick to attack the one-eyed giant Polyphemus: Bloom has only a cigar to flourish in front of a rabid Irish nationalist who attacks him in a pub.

Not only does each of *Ulysses'* eighteen chapters have some reference to a Homeric episode, each had attached to it in Joyce's conception a particular symbol, colour, art (like medicine or law), even a particular organ of the body. Each (after the first half dozen) was also written in a recognisably different style.

The reasons behind the chapter-by-chapter alteration of styles may best be described by saying that Joyce's *Ulysses* is not just the story of Stephen and Bloom; it is a specimen of the nearly infinite number of ways their story *could* be written. The matter of colours, organs and arts is on the other hand reminiscent of the liturgical year in the Roman Catholic Missal, and in a semi-jocular way Joyce thought of *Ulysses* (as many people have of the great literary epics of Homer and Virgil) as a 'sacred' book, mysteriously embodying hidden wisdom and even prophecy.

This latter aspect of Joyce's work became more prominent in his writing after *Ulysses*, between 1922 and 1939. This eventually became one book, *Finnegans Wake*. Like the Bible, the Koran, the Egyptian Book of the Dead, *Finnegans Wake* is about everything: a parable history of the universe from creation to dissolution—and in Joyce's conception, back to creation again, over and over. This 'cyclic' view of history is a comic one, unlike the Christian view, which is a one-way process towards eternal salvation or damnation. Nothing in *Finnegans Wake* happens once and once only. Everything, everybody in the novel (and therefore, in history) has happened before, under different names. To keep before our eyes a sense of this ubiquity and repetitiveness of event and personnel, Joyce hit upon his most radical literary experiment, one so bold that in some quarters he has never been forgiven. Joyce based the language of *Finnegans Wake* on puns of many kinds, principally 'portmanteaux' words and rhythmic echoes of other contexts. *Finnegans Wake* is written largely in the verbal equivalent of photographic double exposure. Here is an unsympathetic description of the artist Shem, Joyce himself—or perhaps, better, of the Joyce-character in history—nearly blind, as Joyce became, in his old age.

4

Be that as it may, but for that light phantastic of his gnose's glow as it slid lucifericiously within an inch of its page (he would touch at its from time to other, the red eye of his fear in saddishness, to ensign the colours by the beerlitz in his mathness and his educandees to outhue to themselves in the cries of girl-gee: gember! inkware! chonchambre! cinsero! zinnzabar! tincture and gin!) Nibs never would have quilled a seriph to sheepskin. By that rosy lampoon's effluvious burning and with help of the simulchronic flush in his pann (a ghinee a ghirk he ghets there!) he scrabbled and scratched and scriobbled and skrevened nameless shamelessness about everybody ever he met, even sharing a precipitation under the idlish tarriers' umbrella of a showerproof wall, while all over up and down the four margins of this rancid Shem stuff the evil-smeller (who was devoted to Uldfadar Sardanapalus) used to stipple endlessly inartistic portraits of himself.

Finnegans Wake, p. 182

The narrator of this diatribe sees only the realistic, critical side of a Joyce : his Joyce writes by the glow from his alcoholic-red nose, a 'lucifericious light, to suggest that his gift is Satanic in origin. The beer-lights (and Joyce was a language teacher at the Berlitz schools for a number of years) in his mathematically-crazed brain give his work its colours. The charge is the same that a student friend made many years before, that he 'scratched' . . . 'nameless shamelessness about everybody ever he met'. (Note the narrator's confusion : a few clauses later he claims Joyce only 'used to stipple endlessly inartistic portraits of himself'.)

'A Portrait of the Artist as a Young Man'

Thus, first and last, Joyce was concerned with the nature and place of 'the artist'. His artist is not a symbol of an Everyman representative of his fellows, but of man apart, defined by his differences from the generality of mankind, at odds with his society. The talents of Joyce's artist are developed and exercised only, as he thinks, in opposition to external pressures like the malice in the voice which describes Shem above. The precise nature of these pressures, in reaction to which the artist makes himself, found categorical expression towards the end of *A Portrait of the Artist*, when Stephen Dedalus is discovering his identity as an artist.

5

—When the soul of a man is born in this country there are nets flung at it to hold it back from flight. You talk to me of nationality, language, religion. I shall try to fly by those nets.

Davin knocked the ashes from his pipe.

—Too deep for me, Stevie, he said. But a man's country comes first. Ireland first, Stevie. You can be a poet or mystic after.

—Do you know what Ireland is? asked Stephen with cold violence. Ireland is the old sow that eats her farrow.
                    A Portrait of the Artist, pp. 211–12

'Language' here means Gaelic, the Irish language, whose use was then being revived, and Irish nationalists were asserting that Irish writers should write in it, rather than in English. Stephen resists this pressure when talking with Davin, a nationalistically-minded student, but when he restates his creed for Cranly, another student, he substitutes for 'language', the 'home'—that is, familial ties—as something the artist must reject in the name of art.

6

—Look here, Cranly, he said. You have asked me what I would do and what I would not do. I will tell you what I will do and what I will not do. I will not serve that in which I no longer believe whether it call itself my home, my fatherland, or my church : and I will try to express myself in some mode of life or art as freely as I can and as wholly as I can, using for my defence the only arms I allow myself to use—silence, exile, and cunning.
                    A Portrait of the Artist, p. 247

Many incidents in the novel combine to bring Stephen to his view of 'the nets' which Ireland 'flings out'. In the following passages we see that injustice at school, family dissention, politics and church authority all appear to Stephen in this light.

7

—You, boy, who are you?
  Stephen's heart jumped suddenly.

—Dedalus, sir.

—Why are you not writing like the others?

—I . . . my . . .

He could not speak with fright.

—Why is he not writing, Father Arnall?

—He broke his glasses, said Father Arnall, and I exempted him from work.

—Broke? What is this I hear? What is this, your name is? said the prefect of studies.

—Dedalus, sir.

—Out here, Dedalus. Lazy little schemer. I see schemer in your face. Where did you break your glasses?

Stephen stumbled into the middle of the class, blinded by fear and haste.

—Where did you break your glasses? repeated the prefect of studies.

—The cinderpath, sir.

—Hoho! The cinderpath! cried the prefect of studies. I know that trick.

Stephen lifted his eyes in wonder and saw for a moment Father Dolan's whitegrey not young face, his baldy whitegrey head with fluff at the sides of it, the steel rims of his spectacles and his nocoloured eyes looking through the glasses. Why did he say he knew that trick?

—Lazy idle little loafer! cried the prefect of studies. Broke my glasses! An old schoolboy trick! Out with your hand this moment!

Stephen closed his eyes and held out in the air his trembling hand with the palm upwards. He felt the prefect of studies touch it for a moment at the fingers to straighten it and then the swish of the sleeve of the soutane as the pandybat was lifted to strike. A hot burning stinging tingling blow like the loud crack of a broken stick made his trembling hand crumple together like a leaf in the fire: and at the sound and the pain scalding tears were driven into his eyes. His whole body was shaking with fright, his arm was shaking and his crumpled burning livid hand shook

13

like a loose leaf in the air. A cry sprang to his lips, a prayer to be let off. But though the tears scalded his eyes and his limbs quivered with pain and fright he held back the hot tears and the cry that scalded his throat.

—Other hand! shouted the prefect of studies.

Stephen drew back his maimed and quivering right arm and held out his left hand. The soutane sleeve swished again as the pandybat was lifted and a loud crashing sound and a fierce maddening tingling burning pain made his hand shrink together with the palms and fingers in a livid quivering mass. The scalding water burst forth from his eyes and, burning with shame and agony and fear, he drew back his shaking arm in terror and burst out into a whine of pain. His body shook with a palsy of fright and in shame and rage he felt the scalding cry come from his throat and the scalding tears falling out of his eyes and down his flaming cheeks.

—Kneel down! cried the prefect of studies.

Stephen knelt down quickly pressing his beaten hands to his sides. To think of them beaten and swollen with pain all in a moment made him feel so sorry for them as if they were not his own but someone else's that he felt sorry for. And as he knelt, calming the last sobs in his throat and feeling the burning tingling pain pressed in to his sides, he thought of the hands which he had held out in the air with the palms up and of the firm touch of the prefect of studies when he had steadied the shaking fingers and of the beaten swollen reddened mass of palm and fingers that shook helplessly in the air.

—Get at your work, all of you, cried the prefect of studies from the door. Father Dolan will be in every day to see if any boy, any lazy idle little loafer wants flogging. Every day. Every day.

The door closed behind him.

A Portrait of the Artist, pp. 87–9

Something has already been said about Joyce's mimicry

14

(or imitation) of his characters' responses or thoughts.

In the three long paragraphs beginning with 'Stephen', what insights into Stephen's reactions do we gain from Joyce's technique?

8

It was his first Christmas dinner and he thought of his little brothers and sisters who were waiting in the nursery, as he had often waited, till the pudding came. The deep low collar and the Eton jacket made him feel queer and oldish: and that morning when his mother had brought him down to the parlour, dressed for mass, his father had cried. That was because he was thinking of his own father. And Uncle Charles had said so too.

Mr Dedalus covered the dish and began to eat hungrily. . . .

—Simon, said Mrs Dedalus, you haven't given Mrs Riordan any sauce.

Mr Dedalus seized the sauceboat.

—Haven't I? he cried. Mrs Riordan, pity the poor blind.

Dante covered her plate with her hands and said:

—No, thanks.

Mr Dedalus turned to uncle Charles.

—How are you off, sir?

—Right as the mail, Simon.

—You, John?

—I'm all right. Go on yourself.

—Mary? Here, Stephen, here's something to make your hair curl.

He poured sauce freely over Stephen's plate and set the boat again on the table. Then he asked uncle Charles was it tender. Uncle Charles could not speak because his mouth was full but he nodded that it was.

—That was a good answer our friend made to the canon. What? said Mr Dedalus.

—I didn't think he had that much in him, said Mr Casey.

—*I'll pay your dues, father, when you cease turning the house of God into a pollingbooth.*

—A nice answer, said Dante, for any man calling himself a catholic to give to his priest.

—They have only themselves to blame, said Mr Dedalus suavely. If they took a fool's advice they would confine their attention to religion.

—It is religion, Dante said. They are doing their duty in warning the people.

—We go to the house of God, Mr Casey said, in all humility to pray to our Maker and not to hear election addresses.

—It is religion, Dante said again. They are right. They must direct their flocks.

—And preach politics from the altar, is it? asked Mr Dedalus.

—Certainly, said Dante. It is a question of public morality. A priest would not be a priest if he did not tell his flock what is right and what is wrong.

Mrs Dedalus laid down her knife and fork, saying:

—For pity sake and for pity sake let us have no political discussion on this day of all days in the year.

—Quite right, ma'am, said uncle Charles. Now Simon, that's quite enough now. Not another word now.

—Yes, yes, said Mr Dedalus quickly.

He uncovered the dish boldly and said:

—Now then, who's for more turkey?

Nobody answered. Dante said:

—Nice language for any catholic to use!

—Mrs Riordan, I appeal to you, said Mrs Dedalus, to let the matter drop now.

Dante turned on her and said:

—And am I to sit hear and listen to the pastors of my church being flouted?

—Nobody is saying a word against them, said Mr Dedalus, so long as they don't meddle in politics.

16

—The bishops and priests of Ireland have spoken, said Dante, and they must be obeyed.

—Let them leave politics alone, said Mr Casey, or the people may leave their church alone.

—You hear? said Dante turning to Mrs Dedalus.

—Mr Casey! Simon! said Mrs Dedalus. Let it end now.

—Too bad! Too bad! said uncle Charles.

What? cried Mr Dedalus. Were we to desert him[1] at the bidding of the English people?

—He was no longer worthy to lead, said Dante. He was a public sinner.

—We are all sinners and black sinners, said Mr Casey coldly.

—*Woe be to the man by whom the scandal cometh!* said Mrs Riordan. *It would be better for him that a millstone were tied about his neck and that he were cast into the depth of the sea rather than that he should scandalize one of these, my least little ones.* That is language of the Holy Ghost.

—And very bad language if you ask me, said Mr Dedalus coolly.

—Simon! Simon! said uncle Charles. The boy. . . .

—O, he'll remember all this when he grows up, said Dante hotly—the language he heard against God and religion and priests in his own home.

—Let him remember too, cried Mr Casey to her from across the table, the language with which the priests and the priests' pawns broke Parnell's heart and hounded him into his grave. Let him remember that too when he grows up.

—Sons of bitches! cried Mr Dedalus. When he was down they turned on him to betray him and rend him like rats in a sewer. Lowlived dogs! And they look it! By Christ, they look it!

[1] Charles Stewart Parnell, Irish political leader, who had died not two months before this dinner See p. 59.

—They behaved rightly, cried Dante. They obeyed their bishops and their priests. Honour to them!

—Well, it is perfectly dreadful to say that not even for one day in the year, said Mrs Dedalus, can we be free from these dreadful disputes! . . .

Dante broke in angrily:

—If we are a priestridden race we ought to be proud of it! They are the apple of God's eye. *Touch them not*, says Christ, *for they are the apple of My eye.*

—And can we not love our country then? asked Mr Casey. Are we not to follow the man that was born to lead us?

—A traitor to his country! replied Dante. A traitor, an adulterer! The priests were right to abandon him. The priests were always the true friends of Ireland.

—Were they, faith? said Mr Casey. . . .

—Right! Right! They were always right! God and morality and religion come first.

Mrs Dedalus, seeing her excitement, said to her:

—Mrs Riordan, don't excite yourself answering them.

—God and religion before everything! Dante cried. God and religion before the world!

Mr Casey raised his clenched fist and brought it down on the table with a crash.

—Very well, then, he shouted hoarsely, if it comes to that, no God for Ireland!

—John! John! cried Mr Dedalus, seizing his guest by the coat sleeve.

Dante started across the table, her cheeks shaking. Mr Casey struggled up from his chair and bent across the table towards her, scraping the air from before his eyes with one hand as though he were tearing aside a cobweb.

—No God for Ireland! he cried. We have had too much God in Ireland. Away with God!

—Blasphemer! Devil! screamed Dante, starting to her feet and almost spitting in his face.

Uncle Charles and Mr Dedalus pulled Mr Casey back

18

into his chair again, talking to him from both sides reasonably. He stared before him out of his dark flaming eyes, repeating:

—Away with God, I say!

Dante shoved her chair violently aside and left the table, upsetting her napkinring which rolled slowly along the carpet and came to rest against the foot of an easychair. Mrs Dedalus rose quickly and followed her towards the door. At the door Dante turned round violently and shouted down the room, her cheeks flushed and quivering with rage:

—Devil out of hell! We won! We crushed him to death! Fiend!

The door slammed behind her.

Mr Casey, freeing his arms from his holders, suddenly bowed his head on his hands with a sob of pain.

—Poor Parnell! he cried loudly. My dead king!

He sobbed loudly and bitterly.

Stephen, raising his terrorstricken face, saw that his father's eyes were full of tears.

A Portrait of the Artist, pp. 71–9

This extract establishes the political and social background for *A Portrait of the Artist as a Young Man*. This background—of a missed opportunity for some form of Irish political independence from England, missed because the Irish people could not agree among themselves to support the policies of Parnell—is behind each of Joyce's novels. Here we see how pro- and anti-Parnell feelings could split families. Later, as Stephen Dedalus approaches manhood, we realise the extent to which his possibilities as an Irish 'artist' are severely curtailed by the demoralisation (as Joyce believed) of the young after the death of Parnell. For Joyce, Irish politics in the 1890s and the first decade of the new century were a dispiriting spectacle of warring factions from the lowest 'ward politics' (after the

American model) to head-in-the-clouds Irish language and Gaelic sports reform.

It is important in absorbing the feel of socio-political dissentions round the Christmas dinner table, from the spiteful to the sentimental, not to lose sight of the human drama. Can you identify who starts this argument, who carries it forward, who attempts to make peace, and so forth? This would be to describe the dramatic rhythm of the scene.

The 'nets' appear to Stephen not only as simple forces of repression but sometimes as avenues of escape. Stephen first experiences, then learns to reject these 'lures'.

9

—I sent for you today, Stephen, because I wished to speak to you on a very important subject.

—Yes, sir.

—Have you ever felt that you had a vocation?

Stephen parted his lips to answer yes and then withheld the word suddenly. The priest waited for the answer and added:

—I mean have you ever felt within yourself, in your soul, a desire to join the order. Think.

—I have sometimes thought of it, said Stephen.

The priest let the blindcord fall to one side and, uniting his hands, leaned his chin gravely upon them, communing with himself.

—In a college like this, he said at length, there is one boy or perhaps two or three boys whom God calls to the religious life. Such a boy is marked off from his companions by his piety, by the good example he shows to others. He is looked up to by them; he is chosen perhaps as prefect by his fellow sodalists. And you, Stephen, have been such a boy in this college, prefect of Our Blessed Lady's sodality.

Perhaps you are the boy in this college whom God designs to call to Himself.

A strong note of pride reinforcing the gravity of the priest's voice made Stephen's heart quicken in response.

—To receive that call, Stephen, said the priest, is the greatest honour that the Almighty God can bestow upon a man. No king or emperor on this earth has the power of the priest of God. No angel or archangel in heaven, no saint, not even the Blessed Virgin herself has the power of a priest of God : the power of the keys, the power to bind and to loose from sin, the power of exorcism, the power to cast out from the creatures of God the evil spirits that have power over them, the power, the authority, to make the great God of Heaven come down upon the altar and take the form of bread and wine. What an awful power, Stephen!

A flame began to flutter again on Stephen's cheek as he heard in this proud address an echo of his own proud musings. How often had he seen himself as a priest wielding calmly and humbly the awful power of which angels and saints stood in reverence! His soul had loved to muse in secret on this desire. He had seen himself, a young and silentmannered priest, entering a confessional swiftly, ascending the altarsteps, incensing, genuflecting, accomplishing the vague acts of the priesthood which pleased him by reason of their semblance of reality and of their distance from it. In that dim life which he had lived through in his musings he had assumed the voices and gestures which he had noted with various priests. He had bent his knee sideways like such a one, he had shaken the thurible only slightly like such a one, his chasuble had swung open like that of such another as he turned to the altar again after having blessed the people. And above all it had pleased him to fill the second place in those dim scenes of his imagining. He shrank from the dignity of celebrant because it displeased him to imagine that all the vague pomp should end in his own person or that the ritual should assign to him so clear and final an office. He longed for the minor sacred offices, to be vested with the tunicle of subdeacon at high mass, to stand aloof from the altar, forgotten by the people, his shoulders covered with a humeral veil, holding the paten within its folds or, when the sacrifice had been accomplished, to stand as deacon in a dalmatic of cloth of gold on the step below the celebrant, his hands joined and his face towards the people, and sing the chant *Ite, missa est*. If ever he had seen himself celebrant it was as in the pictures of the mass in his child's massbook, in a church without worshippers, save for the angel of the sacrifice, at a bare altar and served by an acolyte scarcely more boyish than himself. In vague sacrificial or scaramental acts alone his will seemed drawn to go forth to encounter reality : and it was partly the absence of an appointed rite which had always constrained him to inaction whether he had allowed silence to cover his anger or pride or had suffered only an embrace he longed to give.

A Portrait of the Artist, pp. 174–6

In this extract we can note precisely what it is about a life in the Church which appeals to Stephen. Note the language used to describe how Stephen would feel as a priest. What would be satisfied in Stephen if he became a priest, and, by implication, what would he be saved from?

10

Now, as never before, his strange name seemed to him a prophecy. So timeless seemed the grey warm air, so fluid and impersonal his own mood, that all ages were as one to him. A moment before the ghost of the ancient kingdom of the Danes had looked forth through the vesture of the hazewrapped city. Now, at the name of the fabulous artificer,[2] he seemed to hear the noise of dim waves and to see a winged form flying above the waves and slowly climbing the air. What did it mean? Was it a quaint device opening a page of some medieval book of prophecies and symbols, a hawklike man flying sunward above the sea, a prophecy of the end he had been born to serve and had been following through the mists of childhood and boyhood, a symbol of the artist forging anew in his workshop out of the sluggish matter of the earth a new soaring impalpable imperishable being?

His heart trembled; his breath came faster and a wild spirit passed over his limbs as though he were soaring sunward. His heart trembled in an ecstasy of fear and his soul was in flight. His soul was soaring in an air beyond the world and the body he knew was purified in a breath and delivered of incertitude and made radiant and commingled with the element of the spirit. An ecstasy of flight made radiant his eyes and wild his breath and tremulous and wild and radiant his windswept limbs. . . .

His throat ached with a desire to cry aloud, the cry of a hawk or eagle on high, to cry piercingly of his deliverance to the winds. This was the call of life to his soul not the dull gross voice of the world of duties and despair, not the inhuman voice that had called him to the pale service of the altar. An instant of wild flight had delivered him and the cry of triumph which his lips withheld cleft his brain. . . .

What were they now but the cerements shaken from the body of death—the fear he had walked in night and day, the incertitude that had ringed him round, the shame that had abased him within and without—cerements, the linens of the grave?

His soul had arisen from the grave of boyhood, spurning her graveclothes. Yes! Yes! Yes! He would create proudly

[2] Daedalos of Crete was the mythological inventor of the Labyrinth and of wings for himself and his son Icarus to use to fly home to Greece.

out of the freedom and power of his soul, as the great artificer whose name he bore, a living thing, new and soaring and beautiful, impalpable, imperishable. . . .

There was a long rivulet in the strand: and, as he waded slowly up its course, he wondered at the endless drift of seaweed. Emerald and black and russet and olive, it moved beneath the current, swaying and turning. The water of the rivulet was dark with endless drift and mirrored the highdrifting clouds. The clouds were drifting above him silently and silently the seatangle was drifting below him; and the grey warm air was still: and a new wild life was singing in his veins.

Where was his boyhood now? Where was the soul that had hung back from her destiny, to brood alone upon the shame of her wounds and in her house of squalor and sub-terfuge to queen it in faded cerements and in wreaths that withered at the touch? Or where was he?

He was alone. He was unheeded, happy and near to the wild heart of life. He was alone and young and wilful and wildhearted, alone amid a waste of wild air and brackish waters and the seaharvest of shells and tangle and veiled grey sunlight and gayclad lightclad figures, of children and girls and voices childish and girlish in the air.

A girl stood before him in midstream, alone and still, gazing out to sea. She seemed like one whom magic had changed into the likeness of a strange and beautiful seabird. Her long slender bare legs were delicate as a crane's and pure save where an emerald trail of seaweed had fashioned itself as a sign upon the flesh. Her thighs, fuller and soft-hued as ivory, were bared almost to the hips where the white fringes of her drawers were like featherings of soft white down. Her slateblue skirts were kilted boldly about her waist and dovetailed behind her. Her bosom was as a bird's soft and slight, slight and soft as the breast of some darkplumaged dove. But her long fair hair was girlish: and girlish, and touched with the wonder of mortal beauty, her face.

She was alone and still, gazing out to sea; and when she felt his presence and the worship of his eyes her eyes turned to him in quiet sufferance of his gaze, without shame or wantonness. Long, long she suffered his gaze and then quietly withdrew her eyes from his and bent them towards the stream, gently stirring the water with her foot hither and thither. The first faint noise of gently moving water broke the silence, low and faint and whispering, faint as the bells of sleep; hither and thither, hither and thither: and a faint flame trembled on her cheek.

—Heavenly God! cried Stephen's soul, in an outburst of profane joy.

He turned away from her suddenly and set off across the strand. His cheeks were aflame; his body was aglow; his limbs were trembling. On and on and on and on he strode, far out over the sands, singing wildly to the sea, crying to greet the advent of the life that had cried to him.

Her image had passed into his soul for ever and no word had broken the holy silence of his ecstasy. Her eyes had called him and his soul had leaped at the call. To live, to err, to fall, to triumph, to recreate life out of life!

A Portrait of the Artist, pp. 184–6

This is Stephen's visionary artistic experience, not so much a conversion as a confirmation. It provides him with both a 'mythic' forbear (a sanction) and a vision of the ideal which can yet be found on earth. Both images are 'birds', one of the air, one of the sea.

The initial experience of 'beauty' may be immediate, undefinable, romantic, but Stephen is soon at work analysing it, putting his idea of it—and of the art which can create it—on a firm basis:

II

—To finish what I was saying about beauty, said Stephen, the most satisfying relations of the sensible must therefore correspond to the necessary phases of artistic apprehension. Find these and you find the qualities of universal beauty. Aquinas[3] says: *Ad pulcritudinem tria requiruntur, integritas, consonantia, claritas.* I translate it so: *Three things are needed for beauty, wholeness, harmony and radiance.* Do these correspond to the phases of apprehension? Are you following?

—Of course, I am, said Lynch. If you think I have an excrementitious intelligence run after Donovan and ask him to listen to you.

Stephen pointed to a basket which a butcher's boy had slung inverted on his head.

—Look at that basket, he said.

—I see it, said Lynch.

—In order to see that basket, said Stephen, your mind first of all separates the basket from the rest of the visible universe which is not the basket. The first phase of apprehension is a bounding line drawn about the object to be apprehended. An esthetic image is presented to us either in space or in time. What is audible is presented in time what is visible is presented in space. But, temporal or spatial, the esthetic image is first luminously apprehended as selfbounded and selfcontained upon the immeasurable background of space or time which is not it. You apprehend it as *one* thing. You see it as one whole. You apprehend its wholeness. That is *integritas.*

—Bull's eye! said Lynch, laughing. Go on.

—Then, said Stephen, you pass from point to point, led

[3] St. Thomas Aquinas (c. 1225–1274), Catholic theologian. Author of *Summa Theologica.* Stephen proposes to base his theory of art on an interpretation of Aquinas though he no longer at this time considers himself a member of the Catholic Church.

by its formal lines; you apprehend it as balanced part against part within its limits; you feel the rhythm of its structure. In other words the synthesis of immediate perception is followed by the analysis of apprehension. Having first felt that it is *one* thing you feel now that it is a *thing*. You apprehend it as complex, multiple, divisible, separable, made up of its parts, the result of its parts and their sum, harmonious. That is *consonantia*.

—Bull's eye again! said Lynch wittily. Tell me now what is *claritas* and you win the cigar.

—The connotation of the word, Stephen said, is rather vague. Aquinas uses a term which seems to be inexact. It baffled me for a long time. It would lead you to believe that he had in mind symbolism or idealism, the supreme quality of beauty being a light from some other world, the idea of which the matter is but the shadow, the reality of which it is but the symbol. I thought he might mean that *claritas* is the artistic discovery and representation of the divine purpose in anything or a force of generalisation which would make the esthetic image a universal one, make it outshine its proper conditions. But that is literary talk. I understand it so. When you have apprehended that basket as one thing and have then analysed it according to its form and apprehended it as a thing you make the only synthesis which is logically and esthetically permissible. You see that it is that thing which it is and no other thing. The radiance of which he speaks is the scholastic *quidditas*, the *whatness* of a thing. This supreme quality is felt by the artist when the esthetic image is first conceived in his imagination. The mind in that mysterious instant Shelley likened beautifully to a fading coal. The instant wherein that supreme quality of beauty, the clear radiance of the esthetic image, is apprehended luminously by the mind which has been arrested by its wholeness and fascinated by its harmony is the luminous silent stasis of esthetic pleasure, a spiritual state very like that cardiac condition which the Italian physiologist Luigi Galvani, using a phrase

27

almost as beautiful as Shelley's, called the enchantment of the heart.

Stephen paused and, though his companion did not speak, felt that his words had called up around them a thoughtenchanted silence.

A Portrait of the Artist, pp. 218–20

Stephen's 'theory of art' is a bold and precocious attempt to invent a personal tradition for himself as an artist. He feels he cannot create within the ordinarily available traditions, which he elsewhere calls either 'didactic' or 'pornographic', *i.e.*, arts which either repel or attract. (One can see the rival traditions of realism-naturalism and aestheticism behind his distinction.) *His* art will be neither, but will be 'static', a hard, clear, concrete object which will have no obligation to his environment on the one hand and on the other will not merely be a projection of his own desires.

Armed with both vision and theory, Stephen sets about the serious job of being an 'artist'. The novel closes with a fragment of Stephen's diary, wherein we see a kind of intermediate stage between his life and the art he intends to make out of it. Note the alternation between romantic and realistic modes in the entries. In the entry for April 26th, the first sentence has a realistic, wry twist ('new secondhand'), while the second attempts to remake the 'realism' of the mother's lament into a statement of his own, both by its rhythm and the appended 'Amen'.

12

16 April: Away! Away!

The spell of arms and voices: the white arms of roads, their promise of close embraces and the black arms of tall ships that stand against the moon, their tale of distant nations. They are held out to say: We are alone. Come. And the voices say with them: We are your kinsmen. And the air is thick with their company as they call to me, their kinsman, making ready to go, shaking the wings of their exultant and terrible youth.

26 April: Mother is putting my new secondhand clothes in order. She prays now, she says, that I may learn in my own life and away from home and friends what the heart is and what it feels. Amen. So be it. Welcome, O life! I go to encounter for the millionth time the reality of experience and to forge in the smithy of my soul the uncreated conscience of my race.

27 April: Old father, old artificer, stand me now and ever in good stead.

A Portrait of the Artist, p. 252

With this invocation, *A Portrait of the Artist as a Young Man* ends. Stephen presumably sets off from his native Ireland, testing his new wings, making a decisive effort to free himself from the 'nets' of family, nation and Church.

'Ulysses'

1914 was an *annus mirabilis* for Joyce: he completed the
Portrait, saw *Dubliners* finally published, began *Ulysses*
and wrote his play *Exiles*. When the Great War broke out,
Joyce took his family from Trieste to neutral Switzerland,
and they lived in Zurich until 1919.

Ulysses began, Joyce wrote H. G. Wells, as a 'sequel'
to *A Portrait of the Artist*. In it we discover Stephen
Dedalus returned to Dublin after a time in Paris. He is
living a few miles south of the city in a converted coast-
line tower with two other young men. Here he is, early in
the morning of June 16, 1904, in conversation with one of
them, Buck Mulligan.

13

Buck Mulligan suddenly linked his arm in Stephen's and
walked with him round the tower, his razor and mirror
clacking in the pocket where he had thrust them.

—It's not fair to tease you like that, Kinch,[1] is it? he
said kindly. God knows you have more spirit than any of
them.

[1] Knifeblade—Mulligan's nickname for Stephen.

Parried again. He fears the lancet of my art as I fear that of his. The cold steelpen.

—Cracked lookingglass of a servant.[2] Tell that to the oxy chap[3] downstairs and touch him for a guinea. He's stinking with money and thinks you're not a gentleman. His old fellow made his tin by selling jalap to Zulus or some bloody swindle or other. God, Kinch, if you and I could only work together we might do something for the island. Hellenise it.

Cranly's arm. His arm.

—And to think of your having to beg from these swine. I'm the only one that knows what you are. Why don't you trust me more? What have you up your nose against me? . . . .

They halted, looking towards the blunt cape of Bray Head that lay on the water like the snout of a sleeping whale. Stephen freed his arm quietly.

—Do you wish me to tell you? he asked.

—Yes, what is it? Buck Mulligan answered. I don't remember anything.

He looked in Stephen's face as he spoke. A light wind passed his brow, fanning softly his fair uncombed hair and stirring silver points of anxiety in his eyes.

Stephen, depressed by his own voice, said:

—Do you remember the first day I went to your house after my mother's death?

Buck Mulligan frowned quickly and said:

—What? Where? I can't remember anything. I remember only ideas and sensations. Why? What happened in the name of God?

—You were making tea, Stephen said, and I went across the landing to get more hot water. Your mother

---

[2] Stephen, adapting a remark of Oscar Wilde's, has just called this 'a symbol of Irish art'.
[3] Haines, the third roommate, an Englishman.

and some visitor came out of the drawingroom. She asked you who was in your room.

—Yes? Buck Mulligan said. What did I say? I forget.

—You said, Stephen answered, O, *it's only Dedalus whose mother is beastly dead.*

A flush which made him seem younger and more engaging rose to Buck Mulligan's cheek.

—Did I say that? he asked. Well? What harm is that?

He shook his constraint from him nervously.

—And what is death, he asked, your mother's or yours or my own? You saw only your mother die. I see them pop off every day in the Mater and Richmond and cut up into tripes in the dissecting room. It's a beastly thing and nothing else. It simply doesn't matter. You wouldn't kneel down to pray for your mother on her deathbed when she asked you. Why? Because you have the cursed jesuit strain in you, only it's injected the wrong way. To me it's all a mockery and beastly. Her cerebral lobes are not functioning. She calls the doctor Sir Peter Teazle and picks buttercups off the quilt. Humour her till it's over. You crossed her last wish in death and yet you sulk with me because I don't whinge like some hired mute from Lalouette's. Absurd! I suppose I did say it. I didn't mean to offend the memory of your mother.

He had spoken himself into boldness. Stephen, shielding the gaping wounds which the words had left in his heart, said very coldly:

—I am not thinking of the offence to my mother.

—Of what, then? Buck Mulligan asked.

—Of the offence to me, Stephen answered.

Buck Mulligan swung round on his heel.

—O, an impossible person! he exclaimed.

Ulysses, pp. 6–9

At first the prose alternates between Mulligan's speech

and Stephen's silent thoughts. What is Mulligan's attitude to Stephen here?

Stephen's memory of his dead mother and his remorse at having refused to kneel and pray at her deathbed recur prominently throughout the novel. As does Eveline in the *Dubliners* story of that name, Stephen alternates between obsessive recalls of the latter scene and attempts to free himself from the dead mother's hold over him.

14

A cloud began to cover the sun slowly, shadowing the bay in deeper green. It lay behind him, a bowl of bitter waters. Fergus song: I sang it alone in the house, holding down the long dark chords. Her door was open: she wanted to hear my music. Silent with awe and pity I went to her bedside. She was crying in her wretched bed. For those words, Stephen: love's bitter mystery.

Where now?

Her secrets: old feather fans, tasselled dancecards, powdered with musk, a gaud of amber beads in her locked drawer. A birdcage hung in the sunny window of her house when she was a girl. She heard old Royce sing in the pantomime of Turko the terrible and laughed with others when he sang:

> *I am the boy*
> *That can enjoy*
> *Invisibility.*

Phantasmal mirth, folded away: muskperfumed.

> *And no more turn aside and brood*

Folded away in the memory of nature with her toys. Memories beset his brooding brain. Her glass of water from the kitchen tap when she had approached the sacrament. A cored apple, filled with brown sugar, roasting for

JJ—D

33

her at the hob on a dark autumn evening. Her shapely fingernails reddened by the blood of squashed lice from the children's shirts.

In a dream, silently, she had come to him, her wasted body within its loose graveclothes giving off an odour of wax and rosewood, her breath bent over him with mute secret words, a faint odour of wetted ashes.

Her glazing eyes, staring out of death, to shake and bend my soul. On me alone. The ghostcandle to light her agony. Ghostly light on the tortured face. Her hoarse loud breath rattling in horror, while all prayed on their knees. Her eyes on me to strike me down. *Liliata rutilantium te confessorum turma circumdet: iubilantium te virginum chorus excipiat.*

Ghoul! Chewer of corpses!

No mother. Let me be and let me live.

Ulysses, pp. 9–11

The Latin which Stephen recalls is from the Last Rites administered to the dying Catholic. Phrases from the Latin become a *leitmotif* in the novel, signifying Stephen's memory of the deathbed scene.

In the above passage, Stephen is musing alone. The shift from Joyce's narration to Stephen's thought is only perceptible in the movement from 'he' to 'me'. Often it could be either speaking.

Stephen also feels uneasy over his place among his contemporaries. He resents Mulligan, whom he considers a type of Irishman content to be a paid lackey of England. (In 1904, Ireland was still under British rule.) And he resents the Englishman Haines for his superior manner and his academic interest in the customs of the natives.

An hour later, Stephen is teaching English at a school. In the following extracts we see him first with a student who stays behind after class and then collecting his wages from the headmaster.

15

A stick struck the door and a voice in the corridor called:
—Hockey!

They broke asunder, sidling out of their benches, leaping them. Quickly they were gone and from the lumber-room came the rattle of sticks and clamour of their boots and tongues.

Sargent who alone had lingered came forward slowly, showing an open copybook. His tangled hair and scraggy neck gave witness of unreadiness and through his misty glasses weak eyes looked up pleading. On his cheek, dull and bloodless, a soft stain of ink lay, dateshaped, recent and damp as a snail's bed.

He held out his copybook. The word *Sums* was written on the headline. Beneath were sloping figures and at the foot a crooked signature with blind loops and a blot. Cyril Sargent: his name and seal.

—Mr Deasy told me to write them out all again, he said, and show them to you, sir.

Stephen touched the edges of the book. Futility.

—Do you understand how to do them now? he asked.

—Numbers eleven to fifteen, Sargent answered. Mr Deasy said I was to copy them off the board, sir.

—Can you do them yourself? Stephen asked.

—No, sir.

Ugly and futile: lean neck and tangled hair and a stain of ink, a snail's bed. Yet someone had loved him, borne him in her arms and in her heart. But for her the race of the world would have trampled him under foot, a squashed boneless snail. She had loved his weak watery blood drained from her own. Was that then real? The only true thing in life? . . .

Sitting at his side Stephen solved out the problem. . . . Sargent peered askance through his slanted glasses. Hockey-sticks rattled in the lumberroom: the hollow knock of a ball and calls from the field.

Across the page the symbols moved in grave morrice, in the mummery of their letters, wearing quaint caps of squares and cubes. Give hands, traverse, bow to partner: so: imps of fancy of the Moors. . . .

—Do you understand now? Can you work the second for yourself?

—Yes, sir.

In long shaky strokes Sargent copied the data. Waiting always for a word of help his hand moved faithfully the unsteady symbols, a faint hue of shame flickering behind his dull skin. *Amor matris*: subjective and objective geni- tive.[4] With her weak blood and whey-sour milk she had fed him and hid from sight of others his swaddling bands.

Like him was I, these sloping shoulders, this graceless- ness. My childhood bends beside me. Too far for me to lay a hand there once or lightly. Mine is far and his secret as our eyes. Secrets, silent, stony sit in the dark palaces of both our hearts: secrets weary of their tyranny: tyrants willing to be dethroned.

The sum was done.

—It is very simple, Stephen said as he stood up.

—Yes, sir. Thanks, Sargent answered.

He dried the page with a sheet of thin blottingpaper and carried his copybook back to his desk.

—You had better get your stick and go out to the others, Stephen said as he followed towards the door the boy's graceless form.

—Yes, sir.

In the corridor his name was heard, called from the playfield.

[4] In Latin the phrase means either the love a mother bears for her child or the child's love of its mother.

—Sargent!

—Run on, Stephen said. Mr Deasy is calling you.

Ulysses, pp. 32–4

The presentation of Stephen's unspoken consciousness makes him a more sympathetic character than he would have been had we seen him merely from the outside. Here, the sight of Cyril Sargent calls up in Stephen thoughts about his own childhood and his relationship to his now dead mother. We should note the difference between the restrained sympathy of his speech and the more emotional thought going on behind it.

In the Homeric analogy (see pp. 7–8), Mr. Deasy, Stephen's headmaster, is Nestor, the wise giver of advice to Stephen's Telemachus, the son of Odysseus (Ulysses). An Ulster Irishman and a Protestant, Mr. Deasy—pronounced 'daisy'— is 'very English' in outlook, and he lays down for Stephen yet another path to follow, a very prudent one.

16

—Three twelve, he said. I think you'll find that's right.

—Thank you, sir, Stephen said, gathering the money together with shy haste and putting it all in a pocket of his trousers.

—No thanks at all, Mr Deasy said. You have earned it.

Stephen's hand, free again, went back to the hollow shells. Symbols too of beauty and of power. A lump in my pocket. Symbols soiled by greed and misery.

—Don't carry it like that, Mr Deasy said. You'll pull it out somewhere and lose it. You just buy one of these machines. You'll find them very handy.

Answer something.

—Mine would be often empty, Stephen said.

The same room and hour, the same wisdom: and I the same. Three times now. Three nooses round me here. Well. I can break them in this instant if I will.

—Because you don't save, Mr Deasy said, pointing his finger. You don't know yet what money is. Money is power, when you have lived as long as I have. I know, I know. If youth but knew. But what does Shakespeare say? *Put but money in thy purse.*

—Iago, Stephen murmured.

He lifted his gaze from the idle shells to the old man's stare.

—He knew what money was, Mr Deasy said. He made money. A poet but an Englishman too. Do you know what is the pride of the English? Do you know what is the proudest word you will ever hear from an Englishman's mouth?

The seas' ruler. His seacold eyes[5] looked on the empty bay: history is to blame: on me and on my words, unhating.

—That on his empire, Stephen said, the sun never sets.

—Ba! Mr Deasy cried. That's not English. A French Celt[6] said that. He tapped his savingsbox against his thumbnail.

—I will tell you, he said solemnly, what is his proudest boast. *I paid my way.*

Good man, good man.

—*I paid my way. I never borrowed a shilling in my life.* Can you feel that? *I owe nothing.* Can you?

Mulligan, nine pounds, three pairs of socks, one pair brogues, ties. Curran, ten guineas. McCann, one guinea. Fred Ryan, two shillings. Temple, two lunches. Russell, one guinea, Cousins, ten shillings, Bob Reynolds, half a

---

[5] Englishmen are 'The seas' ruler'. Haines has the 'seacold eyes', and has earlier blamed 'history' for England and Ireland's mutual difficulties.

[6] Perhaps Victor Hugo.

guinea, Kohler, three guineas, Mrs McKernan, five weeks' board.[7] The lump I have is useless.

—For the moment, no, Stephen answered.

Mr Deasy laughed with rich delight, putting back his savingsbox.

—I knew you couldn't, he said joyously. But one day you must feel it. We are a generous people but we must also be just.

—I fear those big words, Stephen said, which make us so unhappy.

Ulysses, pp. 36–8

In the latter portions of *Ulysses*, the narrative voices are varied and themselves become more and more considerably a part of the novel. One of the chapters contains versions of the Dublin story as it might have been told at various periods of English literature. Here is Stephen's situation as John Bunyan might have seen it.

17

But could he not have endeavoured to have found again as in his youth the bottle Holiness that then he lived withal? Indeed not for Grace was not there to find that bottle. Heard he then in that clap the voice of the god Bringforth or, what Calmer[8] said, a hubbub of Phenomenon? Heard? Why, he could not but hear unless he had plugged up the tube Understanding (which he had not done). For through that tube he saw that he was in the land of Phenomenon where he must for a certain one day die as he was like the rest too a passing show. And would he not accept to die like the rest and pass away? By no means would he and make more shows according as men do with wives which Phenomenon has commanded them to do by the book Law. Then wotted he

[7] The list is of Stephen's debts: his salary can hardly reduce it.
[8] Leopold Bloom.

nought of that other land which is called Believe-on-Me,
that is the land of promise which behoves to the king
Delightful and shall be for ever where there is no death
and no birth neither wiving nor mothering at which all
shall come as many as believe on it? Yes, Pious had told
him of that land and Chaste had pointed him to the way
but the reason was that in the way he fell in with a
certain whore of an eyepleasing exterior whose name, she
said, is Bird-in-the-Hand and she beguiled him wrongways
from the true path by her flatteries that she said to him as,
Ho, you pretty man, turn aside hither and I will show you
a brave place, and she lay at him so flatteringly that she
had him in her grot which is named Two-in-the-Bush or,
by some learned, Carnal Concupiscence.

Ulysses, pp. 516-7

Interpret the allegorical names, especially 'Bringforth'
and 'Phenomenon', as they purport to explain Stephen. Do
you think 'the Bunyan view' is Joyce's view of Stephen?

Late in the night, Stephen has found his way to a local
brothel. Joyce composed this chapter as a surrealistic
drama. As what is said in the chapter is not necessarily
what they 'really' said, but a fantasy version of it, we
may expect to meet both the most arbitrary seeming
appearances (here, of Stephen's father Simon as a buzzard
and of his dead mother) and the most penetrating insights
into the depth of Stephen's (and Leopold Bloom's) beings.

18

STEPHEN: Mark me. I dreamt of a watermelon.
ZOE: Go abroad and love a foreign lady.
LYNCH: Across the world for a wife.
FLORRY: Dreams go by contraries.
STEPHEN: (*Extending his arms*) It was here. Street of

harlots. In Serpentine Avenue Beelzebub showed me her, a fubsy widow. Where's the red carpet spread?

BLOOM: (*Approaching Stephen*) Look . . .

STEPHEN: No, I flew. My foes beneath me. And ever shall be. World without end. (*He cries*) Pater! Free!

BLOOM: I say, look . . .

STEPHEN: Break my spirit, will he? *O merde alors!* (*He cries, his vulture talons sharpened*) Hola! Hillyho!

(*Simon Dedalus' voice hilloes in answer, somewhat sleepy but ready*)

SIMON: That's all right. (*He swoops uncertainly through the air, wheeling, uttering cries of heartening, on strong ponderous buzzard wings*) Ho, boy! Are you going to win? Hoop! Pschatt! Stable with those halfcastes. Wouldn't let them within the bawl of an ass. Head up! Keep our flag flying! An eagle gules volant in a field argent displayed. Ulster king at arms! hai hoop! . . .

Ulysses, p. 674

19

STEPHEN: Ho!

(*Stephen's mother, emaciated, rises stark through the floor in leper grey with a wreath of faded orange blossoms and a torn bridal veil, her face worn and noseless, green with grave mould. Her hair is scant and lank. She fixes her bluecircled hollow eyesockets on Stephen and opens her toothless mouth uttering a silent word. A choir of virgins and confessors sing voicelessly.*)

THE CHOIR:

> Liliata rutilantium te confessorum.
> Iubilantium te virginum . . .

(*From the top of a tower Buck Mulligan, in particoloured jester's dress of puce and yellow and clown's cap with curling bell, stands gaping at her, a smoking buttered split scone in his hand*)

BUCK MULLIGAN: She's beastly dead. The pity of it! Mulligan meets the afflicted mother. (*He upturns his eyes*) Mercurial Malachi.

THE MOTHER: (*With the subtle smile of death's madness*) I was once the beautiful May Goulding. I am dead.

STEPHEN: (*Horrorstruck*) Lemur, who are you? What bogeyman's trick is this?

BUCK MULLIGAN: (*Shakes his curling capbell*) The mockery of it! Kinch killed her dogsbody bitchbody. She kicked the bucket. (*Tears of molten butter fall from his eyes into the scone*) Our great sweet mother! *Epi oinopa ponton.*

THE MOTHER: (*Comes nearer, breathing upon him softly her breath of wetted ashes*) All must go through it, Stephen. More women than men in the world. You too. Time will come.

STEPHEN: (*Choking with fright, remorse and horror*) They said I killed you, mother. He offended your memory. Cancer did it, not I. Destiny.

THE MOTHER: (*A green rill of bile trickling from a side of her mouth*) You sang that song to me. *Love's bitter mystery.*

STEPHEN: (*Eagerly*) Tell me the word, mother, if you know now. The word known to all men.

THE MOTHER: Who saved you the night you jumped into the train at Dalkey with Paddy Lee? Who had pity for you when you were sad among the strangers? Prayer is all powerful. Prayer for the suffering souls in the Ursuline manual, and forty days' indulgence. Repent, Stephen.

STEPHEN: The ghoul! Hyena!

THE MOTHER: I pray for you in my other world. Get Dilly to make you that boiled rice every night after your brain work. Years and years I loved you, O my son, my first-born, when you lay in my womb.

ZOE: (*Fanning herself with the grate fan*) I'm melting!

FLORRY: (*Points to Stephen*) Look! He's white.

BLOOM: (*Goes to the window to open it more*) Giddy.

THE MOTHER: (*With smouldering eyes*) Repent! O, the fire of hell!

STEPHEN: (*Panting*) The corpsechewer! Raw head and bloody bones!

THE MOTHER: (*Her face drawing near and nearer, sending out an ashen breath*) Beware! (*She raises her blackened, withered right arm slowly towards Stephen's breast with outstretched fingers*) Beware! God's hand! (*A green crab with malignant red eyes sticks deep its grinning claws in Stephen's heart*)

STEPHEN: (*Strangled with rage*) Shite! (*His features grow drawn and grey and old*)

BLOOM: (*At the window*) What?

STEPHEN: *Ah non, par exemple!* The intellectual imagination! With me all or not at all. *Non serviam!*

FLORRY: Give him some cold water. Wait. (*She rushes out*)

THE MOTHER: (*Wrings her hands slowly, moaning desperately*) O Sacred Heart of Jesus, have mercy on him! Save him from hell, O divine Sacred Heart!

STEPHEN: No! No! No! Break my spirit all of you if you can! I'll bring you all to heel!

THE MOTHER: (*In the agony of her deathrattle*) Have mercy on Stephen, Lord, for my sake! Inexpressible was my anguish when expiring with love, grief and agony on Mount Calvary.

STEPHEN: *Nothung!*

(*He lifts his ashplant high with both hands and smashes the chandelier. Time's livid final flame leaps and, in the following darkness, ruin of all space, shattered glass and toppling masonry.*)

THE GASJET: Pwfungg!

BLOOM: Stop!

LYNCH: (*Rushes forward and seizes Stephen's hand*) Here! Hold on! Don't run amok!

BELLA: Police!

(*Stephen abandoning his ashplant, his head and arms thrown back stark, beats the ground and flees from the room past the whores at the door*)

Ulysses, pp. 680–83

What do the fantasy-appearances of Stephen's parents suggest about his present difficulties?

Leopold Bloom, who has followed Stephen to the brothel, takes him home with him afterwards. The chapter is given as a series of questions and answers.

20

What proposal did Bloom, diambulist, father of Milly, somnambulist, make to Stephen, noctambulist?
To pass in repose the hours intervening between Thursday (proper) and Friday (normal) on an extemporised cubicle in the apartment immediately above the kitchen and immediately adjacent to the sleeping apartment of his host and hostess.

What various advantages would or might have resulted from a prolongation of such extemporisation?
For the guest: security of domicile and seclusion of study. For the host: rejuvenation of intelligence, vicarious satisfaction. For the hostess: disintegration of obsession, acquisition of correct Italian pronunciation.

Why might these several provisional contingencies between a guest and a hostess not necessarily preclude or be precluded by a permanent eventuality of reconciliatory union between a schoolfellow and a jew's daughter?
Because the way to daughter led through mother, the way to mother through daughter. . . .

Was the proposal of asylum accepted?
Promptly inexplicably, with amicability, gratefully it was declined. . . .

Ulysses, pp. 814–5

While the older figures in *Dubliners* tend to be trial 'projections' of Joyce himself—what he might turn into if

44

he were to remain in Dublin—the thirty-eight year old advertising canvasser who balances Stephen Dedalus in *Ulysses* is not. Nor is he that other adult figure, the restrictive parent. Bloom is no pushing, successful man, nor is he one of Dublin's pub-crawling indigents. He has plans, rather too many, and too fancifully conceived, but while their fancifulness is an indication of their ineffectuality, it also indicates the quickness and humour of his mind.

21

Another slice of bread and butter: three, four: right. She didn't like her plate full. Right. He turned from the tray, lifted the kettle off the hob and set it sideways on the fire. It sat there, dull and squat, its spout stuck out. Cup of tea soon. Good. Mouth dry. The cat walked stiffly round a leg of the table with tail on high.

—Mkgnao!

—O, there you are, Mr Bloom said, turning from the fire.

The cat mewed in answer and stalked again stiffly round a leg of the table, mewing. Just how she stalks over my writingtable. Prr. Scratch my head. Prr.

Mr Bloom watched curiously, kindly, the lithe black form. Clean to see: the gloss of her sleek hide, the white button under the butt of her tail, the green flashing eyes. He bent down to her, his hands on his knees.

—Milk for the pussens, he said.

—Mrkgnao! the cat cried.

They call them stupid. They understand what we say better than we understand them. She understands all she wants to. Vindictive to. Wonder what I look like to her. Height of a tower? No, she can jump me.

—Afraid of the chickens she is, he said mockingly. Afraid of the chookchooks. I never saw such a stupid pussens as the pussens.

Cruel. Her nature. Curious mice never squeal. Seem to like it.

—Mrkrgnao! the cat said loudly.

She blinked up out of her avid shameclosing eyes, mewing plaintively and long, showing him her milkwhite teeth. He watched the dark eyeslits narrowing with greed till her eyes were green stones. Then he went to the dresser, took the jug Hanlon's milkman had just filled for him, poured warmbubbled milk on a saucer and set it slowly on the floor.

—Gurrhr! she cried, running to lap.

He watched the bristles shining wirily in the weak light as she tipped three times and licked lightly. Wonder is it true if you clip them they can't mouse after. Why? They shine in the dark, perhaps, the tips. Or kind of feelers in the dark, perhaps.

He listened to her licking lap. Ham and eggs, no. No good eggs with this drouth. Want pure fresh water. Thursday: not a good day either for a mutton kidney at Buckley's. Fried with butter, a shake of pepper. Better a pork kidney at Dlugacz's. While the kettle is boiling. She lapped slower, then licking the saucer clean. Why are their tongues so rough? To lap better, all porous holes. Nothing she can eat? He glanced round him. No.

On quietly creaky boots he went up the staircase to the hall, paused by the bedroom door. She might like something tasty. Thin bread and butter she likes in the morning.

Ulysses, pp. 65–6

'She' is mostly the cat, but sometimes Bloom's wife Molly. The ambiguity suggests Bloom is meditating as much on femininity (as he knows it) as on cats. Joyce develops the relationship between Bloom and his wife with deft dialogue.

22

Two letters and a card lay on the hallfloor. He stopped and gathered them. Mrs Marion Bloom. His quick heart slowed at once. Bold hand. Mrs Marion.

—Poldy!

Entering the bedroom he halfclosed his eyes and walked through warm yellow twilight towards her tousled head.

—Who are the letters for?

He looked at them. Mullingar. Milly.

—A letter for me from Milly, he said carefully, and a card to you. And a letter for you.

He laid her card and letter on the twill bedspread near the curve of her knees.

—Do you want the blind up?

Letting the blind up by gentle tugs halfway his backward eye saw her glance at the letter and tuck it under her pillow.

—That do? he asked, turning.

She was reading the card, propped on her elbow.

—She got the things, she said.

He waited till she had laid the card aside and curled herself back slowly with a snug sigh.

—Hurry up with that tea, she said. I'm parched.

—The kettle is boiling, he said.

But he delayed to clear the chair: her striped petticoat, tossed soiled linen: and lifted all in an armful on to the foot of the bed.

As he went down the kitchen stairs she called:

—Poldy!

—What?

—Scald the teapot.

Ulysses, pp. 74–5

Elsewhere full comment on his own creation, here Joyce is laconic. Two points are at issue: that Bloom has received a letter and Molly only a card from their daughter, who is away for the summer working, and that Molly has received a letter she does not want to open with Bloom present. In fact, as Bloom knows, it is a letter from Molly's manager (she is a singer), Blazes Boylan, and the letter confirms a tryst the two have arranged for that afternoon under cover of a meeting to discuss concert plans. A few hours later, Bloom is thinking (as he does so often during the day) of that meeting.

23

He's coming in the afternoon. Her songs.

Plasto's. Sir Philip Crampton's memorial fountain bust. Who was he?

—How do you do? Martin Cunningham said, raising his palm to his brow in salute.

—He doesn't see us, Mr Power said. Yes, he does. How do you do?

—Who? Mr Dedalus asked.

—Blazes Boylan, Mr Powers said. There he is airing his quiff.

Just that moment I was thinking.

Mr Dedalus bent across to salute. From the door of the Red Bank the white disc of a straw hat flashed reply: passed.

Mr Bloom reviewed the nails of his left hand, then those of his right hand. The nails, yes. Is there anything more in him that they she sees? Fascination. Worst man in Dublin. That keeps him alive. They sometimes feel what a person is. Instinct. But a type like that. My nails. I am just looking at them: well pared. And after: thinking alone. Body getting a bit softy. I would notice that from remembering. What causes that I suppose the skin can't contract quickly enough when the flesh falls off. But the shape is there. The shape is there still. Shoulders. Hips.

Plump. Night of the dance dressing. Shift stuck between the cheeks behind.

He clasped his hands between his knees and, satisfied, sent his vacant glance over their faces.

Mr Power asked:

—How is the concert tour getting on, Bloom?

—O very well, Mr Bloom said. I hear great accounts of it. It's a good idea, you see . . .

—Are you going yourself?

—Well no, Mr Bloom said. In point of fact I have to go down to the county Clare on some private business. You see the idea is to tour the chief towns. What you lose on one you can make up on the other.

Ulysses, pp. 114–5

Can you comment on the 'irrelevance' of what Bloom thinks of both before and after Boylan is brought to his notice?

Mr. Bloom and his acquaintances including Stephen Dedalus's father Simon, are here riding together in a funeral carriage, going to the interment of an old crony, Paddy Dignam. A few moments earlier, Bloom had noticed Stephen in the street.

24

All watched awhile through their windows caps and hats lifted by passers. Respect. The carriage swerved from the tramtrack to the smoother road past Watery lane. Mr Bloom at gaze saw a lithe young man, clad in mourning, a wide hat.

—There's a friend of yours gone by, Dedalus, he said.

—Who is that?

—Your son and heir.

—Where is he? Mr Dedalus said, stretching over across.

The carriage, passing the open drains and mounds of rippedup roadway before the tenement houses, lurched round the corner and, swerving back to the tramtrack, rolled on noisily with chattering wheels. Mr Dedalus fell back, saying:

—Was that Mulligan cad with him? His *fidus Achates*?

—No, Mr Bloom said. He was alone.

—Down with his aunt Sally, I suppose, Mr Dedalus said, the Goulding faction, the drunken little costdrawer and Crissie, papa's little lump of dung, the wise child that knows her own father.

Mr Bloom smiled joylessly on Ringsend road. Wallace Bros the bottleworks. Dodder bridge.

Richie Goulding and the legal bag. Goulding, Collis and Ward he calls the firm. His jokes are getting a bit damp. Great card he was. Waltzing in Stamer street with Ignatius Gallaher on a Sunday morning, the landlady's two hats pinned on his head. Out on the rampage all night. Beginning to tell on him now: that backache of his, I fear. Wife ironing his back. Thinks he'll cure it with pills. All breadcrumbs they are. About six hundred per cent profit.

—He's in with a lowdown crowd, Mr Dedalus snarled. That Mulligan is a contaminated bloody doubledyed ruffian by all accounts. His name stinks all over Dublin. But with the help of God and His blessed mother I'll make it my business to write a letter one of those days to his mother or his aunt or whatever she is that will open her eye as wide as a gate. I'll tickle his catastrophe believe you me.

He cried above the clatter of the wheels.

—I won't have her bastard of a nephew ruin my son. A counter-jumper's son. Selling tapes in my cousin, Peter Paul M'Swiney's. Not likely.

He ceased. Mr Bloom glanced from his angry moustache to Mr Power's mild face and Martin Cunningham's eyes and beard, gravely shaking. Noisy selfwilled man. Full of his son. He is right. Something to hand on. If little Rudy had lived. See him grow up. Hear his voice in the house.

Walking beside Molly in an Eton suit. My son. Me in his eyes. Strange feeling it would be. From me. Just a chance.

Ulysses, pp. 109–10

This section defines the differences between Bloom and Simon Dedalus. Bloom's reaction to Dedalus's tirade is complex, and proceeds from instinctive dislike of the man to admission that 'He is right' and a certain sympathy with him. This movement of mind is typical of Bloom, who is capable of responding sympathetically under adverse conditions. But typical, too, is the way he allows his sympathy to spill over into a fantasy about his own son, 'little Rudy', who died in the second week of infancy, nine years before.

In the late afternoon we see Bloom again in company, having called in at a pub to keep an appointment. The chapter has a new narrator, who relates unsympathetically how 'the citizen', an ardent Irish Nationalist, picked a fight with Bloom.

25

But begob I was just lowering the heel of the pint when I saw the citizen getting up to waddle to the door, puffing and blowing with the dropsy and he cursing the curse of Cromwell on him, bell, book and candle in Irish, spitting and spatting out of him and Joe and little Alf round him like a leprechaun trying to peacify him.

—Let me alone, says he.

And begob he got as far as the door and they holding him and he bawls out of him:

—Three cheers for Israel!

Arrah, sit down on the parliamentary side of your arse for Christ's sake and don't be making a public exhibition of yourself. Jesus, there's always some bloody clown or other kicking up a bloody murder about bloody nothing. Gob, it'd turn the porter sour in your guts, so it would.

51

And all the ragamuffins and sluts of the nation round the door and Martin telling the jarvey to drive ahead and the citizen bawling and Alf and Joe at him to whisht and he on his high horse about the jews and the loafers calling for a speech and Jack Power trying to get him to sit down on the car and hold his bloody jaw and a loafer with a patch over his eye starts singing *If the man in the moon was a jew, jew, jew* and a slut shouts out of her:

—Eh, mister! Your fly is open, mister!

And says he:

—Mendelssohn was a jew and Karl Marx and Mercadante and Spinoza. And the Saviour was a jew and his father was a jew. Your God.

—He had no father, says Martin. That'll do now. Drive ahead.

—Whose God? says the citizen.

—Well, his uncle was a jew, says he. Your God was a jew. Christ was a jew like me.

Gob, the citizen made a plunge back into the shop.

—By Jesus, says he, I'll brain that bloody jewman for using the holy name. By Jesus, I'll crucify him so I will. Give us that biscuitbox here.

—Stop! Stop! says Joe.

A large and appreciative gathering of friends and acquaintances from the metropolis and greater Dublin assembled in their thousands to bid farewell to Nagyaságos uram Lipóti Virag, late of Messrs Alexander Thom's, printers to His Majesty, on the occasion of his departure for the distant clime of Százharminczbrojúgulyás-Dugulás (Meadow of Murmuring Waters). The ceremony which went off with great *éclat* was characterised by the most affecting cordiality. An illuminated scroll of ancient Irish vellum, the work of Irish artists, was presented to the distinguished phenomenologist on behalf of a large section of the community and was accompanied by the gift of a silver casket, tastefully executed in the style of ancient Celtic ornament, a work which reflects every credit on the makers, Messrs

Jacob *agus* Jacob. The departing guest was the recipient of a hearty ovation, many of those who were present being visibly moved when the select orchestra of Irish pipes struck up the wellknown strains of *Come back to Erin*, followed immediately by *Rakoczy's March*. . . .

Gob, the devil wouldn't stop him till he got hold of the bloody tin anyhow and out with him and little Alf hanging on to his elbow and he shouting like a stuck pig, as good as any bloody play in the Queen's royal theatre.

—Where is he till I murder him?

And Ned and J. G. paralysed with the laughing.

—Bloody wars, says I, I'll be in for the last gospel.

But as luck would have it the jarvey got the nag's head round the other way and off with him.

—Hold on, citizen, says Joe. Stop.

Begob he drew his hand and made a swipe and let fly. Mercy of God the sun was in his eyes or he'd have left him for dead. Gob, he near sent it into the county Longford. The bloody nag took fright and the old mongrel after the car like bloody hell and all the populace shouting and laughing and the old tinbox clattering along the street.

The catastrophe was terrific and instantaneous in its effect. The observatory of Dunsink registered in all eleven shocks, all of the fifth grade of Mercalli's scale, and there is no record extant of a similar seismic disturbance in our island since the earthquake of 1534, the year of the rebellion of Silken Thomas. The epicentre appears to have been that part of the metropolis which constitutes the Inn's Quay ward and parish of Saint Michan covering a surface of fortyone acres, two roods and one square pole or perch. All the lordly residences in the vicinity of the palace of justice were demolished and that noble edifice itself, in which at the time of the catastrophe important legal debates were in progress, is literally a mass of ruins beneath which it is to be feared all the occupants have been buried alive. From the reports of eyewitnesses it transpires that the seismic waves were accompanied by a violent atmospheric perturbation of cyclonic character. . . . Other eyewitnesses depose that they observed an incandescent object of enormous proportions hurtling through the atmosphere at a terrifying velocity in a trajectory directed south west by west. Messages of condolence and sympathy are being hourly received from all parts of the different continents and the sovereign pontiff has been graciously pleased to decree that a special *missa pro defunctis* shall be celebrated simultaneously by the ordinaries of each and every cathedral church of all the episcopal dioceses subject to the spiritual authority of the Holy See in suffrage of the souls of those faithful departed who have been so unexpectedly called away from our midst. The work of salvage, removal of *débris* human remains etc has been entrusted to Messrs Michael Meade and Son, 159, Great Brunswick Street and Messrs T. C. Martin, 77, 78, 79 and 80, North Wall, assisted by the men and officers of the Duke of Cornwall's light infantry. . . .

You never saw the like of it in all your born puff. Gob, if he got that lottery ticket on the side of his poll he'd remember the gold cup, he would so, but begob the citizen would have been lagged for assault and battery and Joe for aiding and abetting. The jarvey saved his life by furious driving as sure as God made Moses. What? O, Jesus, he did. And he let a volley of oaths after him.

—Did I kill him, says he, or what?

And he shouting to the bloody dog.

—After him, Garry! After him, boy!

And the last we saw was the bloody car rounding the corner and old sheepface on it gesticulating and the bloody mongrel after it with his lugs back for all he was bloody well worth to tear him limb from limb. Hundred to five! Jesus, he took the value of it out of him, I promise you.

When, lo, there came about them all a great brightness and they beheld the chariot wherein He stood ascend to heaven. And they beheld Him in the chariot, clothed upon in the glory of the brightness, having raiment as of the sun, fair as the moon and terrible that for awe they durst not look upon Him. And there came a voice out of heaven, calling: *Elijah! Elijah!* And he answered with a main cry: *Abba! Adonai!* And they beheld Him even Him, ben Bloom Elijah, amid clouds of angels ascend to the glory of the brightness at an angle of fortyfive degrees over Donohoe's in Little Green Street like a shot off a shovel.

Ulysses, pp. 444-9

This is the 'Cyclops' episode (in the Homeric parody) and Ulysses-Bloom is pitted against the Cyclops-'citizen'. Bloom's own mind now clearly established for us, Joyce is here embarked on that stylistic experimentation which characterises the latter portions of *Ulysses* and in this passage there are three distinct parodic sections which set the present action in various heroic ('cyclopean') lights, two pseudo-newspaper reports—in the then florid style of popular journalism—and one biblical. Each inflates the issue at hand, but with what effect? Who or what is being got at by these parodies?

The same question—what is the effect of Joyce's parody-styles as a commentary on his Dublin action—may be asked about the next extract, from the hospital chapter of *Ulysses*: late in the evening, Bloom joins Stephen and his medical companions round a table at a Dublin maternity hospital. (Bloom's meeting with Stephen is thus accidental: he has stopped by to inquire after a woman in labour.) In the *style* Joyce chose to suit his subject in this chapter—the recapitulation of English prose styles to match the stages of human gestation—the naming of the company and Leopold Bloom's interest in Stephen come out in a parody of the chivalric style of Sir Thomas Malory.

55

26

Now let us speak of that fellowship that was there to the intent to be drunken an they might. There was a sort of scholars along either side the board, that is to wit, Dixon yclept junior of saint Mary Merciable's with other his fellows Lynch and Madden, scholars of medicine, and the franklin that hight Lenehan and one from Alba Longa, one Crotthers, and young Stephen that had mien of a frere that was at head of the board and Costello that men clepen Punch Costello all long of a mastery of him erewhile gested (and of all them, reserved young Stephen, he was the most drunken that demanded still of more mead) and beside the meek sir Leopold. But on young Malachi they waited for that he promised to have come and such as intended to no goodness said how he had broke his avow. And sir Leopold sat with them for he bore fast friendship to sir Simon and to this his son young Stephen and for that his languor becalmed him there after longest wanderings insomuch as they feasted him for that time in the honourablest manner. Ruth red him, love led on with will to wander, loth to leave. . . .

Ulysses, p. 507

The chapter in which Bloom follows Stephen to a Dublin brothel is the longest in the novel. It is written in the form of a play, with dialogue and extended stage directions. This 'play' is a surrealistic fantasia *imagined* by Joyce *about* his characters, who probably never said, as it were, what he attributes to them.

As Bloom enters Dublin's 'red-light' district he is confronted by the apparition of his long-dead father, Rudolph Virag, who committed suicide by poison.

27

(*The retriever approaches sniffling, nose to the ground. A sprawled form sneezes. A stooped bearded figure appears garbed in the long caftan of an elder in Zion and a smoking cap with magenta tassels. Horned spectacles hang down at the wings of the nose. Yellow poison streaks are on the drawn face.)*

RUDOLPH: Second halfcrown waste money today. I told you not go with drunken goy ever. So. You catch no money.

BLOOM: *(Hides the crubeen and trotter behind his back and, crestfallen, feels warm and cold feetmeat)* Ja, ich weiss, papachi.

RUDOLPH: What you making down this place? Have you no soul? *(With feeble vulture talons he feels the silent face of Bloom)* Are you not my son Leopold, the grandson of Leopold? Are you not my dear son Leopold who left the house of his father and left the god of his fathers Abraham and Jacob?

Ulysses, pp. 568–9

It is in this chapter that Joyce can give free rein to Bloom's schemes for private and public improvement. (The implication is that ordinarily these schemes never become this articulate and remain only possibilities in the 'ideal' Bloom here presented.) But while the imaginary Dubliners of Joyce's surrealist fantasy-drama first applaud 'Bloom's' ideas, they soon, at the prompting of the priest Father Farley, turn on him in the classic pattern of the Irish betrayal of her leaders.

28

BLOOM: My beloved subjects, a new era is about to dawn. I, Bloom, tell you verily it is even now at hand. Yea, on the word of a Bloom, ye shall ere long enter into the golden city which is to be, the new Bloomusalem in the Nova Hibernia of the future.

(*Thirtytwo workmen wearing rosettes, from all the counties of Ireland, under the guidance of Derwan the builder, construct the new Bloomusalem. It is a colossal edifice, with crystal roof, built in the shape of a huge pork kidney, containing forty thousand rooms. In the course of its extension several buildings and monuments are demolished. Government offices are temporarily transferred to railway sheds. Numerous houses are razed to the ground. The inhabitants are lodged in barrels and boxes, all marked in red with letters: L. B. Several paupers fall from a ladder. A part of the walls of Dublin, crowded with loyal sightseers, collapses.*)

THE SIGHTSEERS: (*Dying*) Morituri te salutant. (*They die*). . . .

BLOOM: I stand for the reform of municipal morals and the plain ten commandments. New worlds for old. Union of all, jew, moslem and gentile. Three acres and a cow for all children of nature. Saloon motor hearses. Compulsory manual labour for all. All parks open to the public day and night. Electric dishscrubbers. Tuberculosis, lunacy, war and mendicancy must now cease. General amnesty, weekly carnival, with masked licence, bonuses for all, esperanto the universal brotherhood. No more patriotism of barspongers and dropsical impostors. Free money, free love and a free lay church in a free lay state. . . .

FATHER FARLEY: He is an episcopalian, an agnostic, an anythingarian seeking to overthrow our holy faith.

MRS. RIORDAN: (*Tears up her will*) I'm disappointed in you! You bad man!

MOTHER GROGAN: (*Removes her boot to throw it at Bloom*) You beast! You abominable person! . . .

THE VEILED SIBYL: (*Enthusiastically*) I'm a Bloomite and I glory in it. I believe in him in spite of all. I'd give my life for him, the funniest man on earth.

BLOOM: (*Winks at the bystanders*) I bet she's a bonny lassie.

THEODORE PUREFOY: (*In fishing cap and oilskin jacket*)

He employs a mechanical device to frustrate the sacred ends of nature.

THE VEILED SIBYL: (*Stabs herself*) My hero god! (*She dies*) (*Many most attractive and enthusiastic women also commit suicide by stabbing, drowning, drinking prussic acid, aconite, arsenic, opening their veins, refusing food, casting themselves under steamrollers, from the top of Nelson's Pillar, into the great vat of Guinness's brewery, asphyxiating themselves by placing their heads in gas ovens, hanging themselves in stylish garters, leaping from windows of different storeys*)

ALEXANDER J. DOWIE: (*Violently*) Fellowchristians and anti-Bloomites, the man called Bloom is from the roots of hell, a disgrace to christian men. A fiendish libertine from his earliest years this stinking goat of Mendes gave precocious signs of infantile debauchery recalling the cities of the plain, with a dissolute granddam. This vile hypocrite, bronzed with infamy, is the white bull mentioned in the Apocalypse. A worshipper of the Scarlet Woman, intrigue is the very breath of his nostrils. The stake faggots and the caldron of boiling oil are for him. Caliban!

THE MOB: Lynch him! Roast him! He's as bad as Parnell was. Mr Fox!

(*Mother Grogan throws her boot at Bloom. Several shopkeepers from upper and lower Dorset street throw objects of little or no commercial value, hambones, condensed milk tins, unsaleable cabbage, stale bread, sheeps' tails, odd pieces of fat.*)

Ulysses, pp. 606–12

The Irish Parliamentary leader, Charles Stewart Parnell, was similarly treated after being denounced by the Irish Catholic clergy as an adulterer. (Mr. Fox was a pseudonym he used when visiting his mistress.)

Once the 'hero god' Bloom is 'lynched' by the crowd, the scenario shifts to more private affairs. All day Bloom has refused to face the question of his own wife's adultery that afternoon. Now Joyce makes him face it with vengeance, acting as a lackey at the assignation.

29

BOYLAN: (*Jumps surely from the car and calls loudly for all to hear*) Hello, Bloom! Mrs Bloom up yet?

BLOOM: (*In a flunkey's plum plush coat and kneebreeches, buff stockings and powdered wig*) I'm afraid not, sir, the last articles . . .

BOYLAN: (*Tosses him sixpence*) Here, to buy yourself a gin and splash. (*He hangs his hat smartly on a peg of Bloom's antlered head*) Show me in. I have a little private business with your wife. You understand?

BLOOM: Thank you, sir. Yes, sir, Madam Tweedy is in her bath, sir.[9]

MARION: He ought to feel himself highly honoured. (*She plops splashing out of the water*) Raoul, darling, come and dry me. I'm in my pelt. Only my new hat and a carriage sponge.

BOYLAN: (*A merry twinkle in his eye*) Topping!

Ulysses, pp. 669–70

Despite the abyss of depravity in which this plunges him, shortly thereafter he appears as the old Bloom as he hovers nervously over Stephen (who has been knocked unconscious by a drunken soldier). His feelings of pity and concern mingle with his own feelings of loss over the son Rudy who didn't live and whose death has cast a blight over his relations with his wife.

30

BLOOM: Poetry. Well educated. Pity. (*He bends again and undoes the buttons of Stephen's waistcoat*) To breathe. (*He

[9] Marion Tweedy, Mrs. (Molly) Bloom's maiden name.

*brushes the wood shavings from Stephen's clothes with
light hands and fingers)* One pound seven. Not hurt anyhow. (*He listens*) What!

> . . . shadows . . . the woods.
> . . . white breast . . . dim . . .[10]

(*He stretches out his arms, sighs again and curls his body.
Bloom holding his hat and ashplant stands erect. A dog
barks in the distance. Bloom tightens and loosens his grip
on the ashplant. He looks down on Stephen's face and
form.*)
BLOOM: (*Communes with the night*) Face reminds me of
his poor mother. In the shady wood. The deep white breast.
Ferguson, I think I caught. A girl. Some girl. Best thing
could happen him . . . (*He murmurs*) . . . swear that
I will always hail, ever conceal, never reveal, any part
or parts, art or arts . . . (*He murmurs*) in the rough sands
of the sea . . . a cabletow's length from the shore . . .
where the tide ebbs . . . and flows . . .
(*Silent, thoughtful, alert, he stands on guard, his fingers at
his lips in the attitude of secret master. Against the dark
wall a figure appears slowly, a fairy boy of eleven, a
changeling, kidnapped, dressed in an Eton suit with glass
shoes and a little bronze helmet, holding a book in his hand.
He reads from right to left inaudibly, smiling, kissing the
page.*)
BLOOM: (*Wonderstruck, calls inaudibly*) Rudy!
RUDY: (*Gazes unseeing into Bloom's eyes and goes on reading, kissing, smiling. He has a delicate mauve face. On his
suit he has diamond and ruby buttons. In his free left hand
he holds a slim ivory cane with a violet bowknot. A white
lambkin peeps out of his waistcoat pocket.*)

Ulysses, pp. 702–3

---

[10] Stephen, nearly unconscious, is murmuring phrases from a
poem by W. B. Yeats. His mother, lying on her deathbed, used
to ask Stephen to sing it to her in its musical setting. See p. 33.

Bloom's subsequent rescue of Stephen Dedalus from a scrap suggests that an occasion has presented itself whereby Stephen might, with proper handling, become a substitute son for Bloom. This hope is, of course, of a piece with many of Bloom's other desires, and Joyce treats Bloom's attempt to manipulate Stephen into a relationship with him ironically by writing the entire chapter which follows the brothel scene in *cliches*.

31

Anyhow, upon weighing the pros and cons, getting on for one as it was, it was high time to be retiring for the night. The crux was it was a bit risky to bring him home as eventualities might possibly ensue (somebody having a temper of her own sometimes) and spoil the hash altogether as on the night he misguidedly brought home a dog (breed unknown) with a lame paw, not that the cases were either identical or the reverse, though he had hurt his hand too, to Ontario Terrace, as he very distinctly remembered, having been there, so to speak. On the other hand it was altogether far and away too late for the Sandymount or Sandycove suggestion so that he was in some perplexity as to which of the two alternatives . . . Everything pointed to the fact that it behoved him to avail himself to the full of the opportunity, all things considered. His initial impression was that he was a bit standoffish or not over effusive but it grew on him someway. For one thing he mightn't what you call jump at the idea, if approached, and what mostly worried him was he didn't know how to lead up to it or word it exactly, supposing he did entertain the proposal, as it would afford him very great personal pleasure if he would allow him to help to put coin in his way or some wardrobe, if found suitable. At all events he wound up by concluding, eschewing for the nonce hidebound precedent, a cup of Epp's cocoa and a shakedown for the night plus the use of a rug or two and overcoat doubled into a pillow. At least he would be in safe hands and as warm as a toast on a trivet. He failed to perceive any very vast amount of harm in that always with the proviso no rumpus of any sort was kicked up.

Ulysses, p. 765

In the penultimate chapter Stephen turns down Bloom's offer of a night's lodging and goes off into the night. Joyce 'reduces' Bloom's reactions after Stephen has left, in the question-and-answer style of the chapter.

32

Alone. what did Bloom feel?
The cold of interstellar space, thousands of degrees below freezing point or the absolute zero of Farenheit, Centigrade or Réumur: the incipient intimations of proximate dawn.

Ulysses, p. 827

'Alone', Bloom mulls over his long day. Despite his many resolutions, quickly taken, quickly abandoned, to either confront Molly and Boylan with his knowledge or to leave her, he finds himself 'home', with an unfaithful 'Penelope'. Joyce offers an analysis in the style of a clinical report.

33

With what antagonistic sentiments were his subsequent reflections affected?
Envy, jealousy, abnegation, equanimity. . . .
Equanimity?
As natural as any and every natural act of a nature expressed or understood executed in natured nature by natural creatures in accordance with his, her and their

63

natured natures, of dissimilar similarity. As not as cala-
mitous as a cataclysmic annihilation of the planet in con-
sequence of collision with a dark sun. As less reprehensible
than theft, highway robbery, cruelty to children and
animals, obtaining money under false pretences, forgery,
embezzlement, misappropriation of public money, betrayal of public trust, malingering, mayhem, corruption
of minors, criminal libel, blackmail, contempt of court,
arson, treason, felony, mutiny on the high seas, trespass,
burglary, jailbreaking, practice of unnatural vice, desertion
from armed forces in the field, perjury, poaching, usury,
intelligence with the king's enemies, impersonation, criminal assault, manslaughter, wilful and premeditated murder.
As not more abnormal than all other altered processes of
adaptation to altered conditions of existence, resulting in a
reciprocal equilibrium between the bodily organism and its
attendant circumstances, foods, beverages, acquired habits,
indulged inclinations, significant disease. As more than
inevitable, irreparable.

Ulysses, pp. 864–5

So in the end, Bloom 'accepts' the situation, acting
either in a cowardly manner or in a brave and heroic one,
depending on your point of view. Joyce takes no sides here,
though he presents many, his various 'styles' enforcing
different attitudes. The style of the present chapter he
himself called in the list of *Ulysses*' styles he made for a
friend 'impersonal', and we fade out on a Bloom mulling
over, 'the futility of triumph or protest or vindication :
the inanity of extolled virtue : the lethargy of nescient
matter : the apathy of the stars.'

Joyce put in a large egg-shaped full-stop after this chapter, to signify that in a way his novel was finished, though
it had one chapter yet to go. In that final chapter we do not
see any further action by Bloom or Stephen, only the cogi-

tations of Bloom's wife Molly as she lies next to him, drop-ing off to sleep. This chapter, which is known as Molly Bloom's 'soliloquy', has no punctuation, but runs on and on at a level of consciousness below that which we have marked in the waking Bloom and Stephen. Perhaps this is the way women 'think' (according to Joyce), or perhaps Bloom and Stephen think like this, too, when they are nearly asleep. In any case, the chapter provides a coda to Bloom's hopes and fears, and we are left to judge how likely it is that he will resolve his difficulties satisfactorily with a woman like this.

34

Bartell dArcy too that he used to make fun of when he commenced kissing me on the choir stairs after I sang Gounods *Ave Maria* what are we waiting for O my heart kiss me straight on the brow and part which is my brown part he was pretty hot for all his tinny voice too my low notes he was always raving about if you can believe him I liked the way he used his mouth singing then he said wasnt it terrible to do that there in a place like that I dont see anything so terrible about it Ill tell him about that some day not now and surprise him ay and Ill take him there and show him the very place too we did it so now there you are like it or lump it he thinks nothing can happen without him knowing he hadnt an idea about my mother till we were engaged otherwise hed never have got me so cheap as he did he was 10 times worse himself anyhow begging me to give him a tiny bit cut off my drawers that was the evening coming along Kenilworth square he kissed me in the eye of my glove and I had to take it off asking me questions is it permitted to inquire the shape of my bed-room so I let him keep it as if I forgot it to think of me when I saw him slip it into his pocket of course hes mad on the subject of drawers thats plain to be seen always skeezing at those brazenfaced things on the bicycles with their skirts blowing up to their navels even when Milly and I were out with him at the open air fete that one in the cream muslin stading right against the sun so he could see every atom she had on

Ulysses, pp. 881–2

The course Molly's consciousness takes is interesting to follow: she remembers past amours, enjoys the memory, begins to feel guilty, blames Bloom, exonerates herself, and so over again. As she thinks on, her memories of the past centre on her only really happy time, the period of courting before she married Bloom.

35

I never thought that would be my name Bloom when I used to write it in print to see how it looked on a visiting card or practising for the butcher and oblige M Bloom youre looking blooming Josie used to say after I married him well its better than Breen or Briggs does brig or those awful names with bottom in them Mrs Ramsbottom or some other kind of a bottom Mulvey I wouldnt go mad about either or suppose I divorced him Mrs Boylan my mother whoever she was might have given me a nicer name the Lord knows after the lovely one she had Lunita Laredo the fun we had running along Willis road to Europa point twisting in and out all round the other side of Jersey they were shaking and dancing about in my blouse like Millys little ones now when she runs up the stairs I loved looking down at them I was jumping up at the pepper trees and the white poplars pulling the leaves off and throwing them at him he went to India he was to write the voyages those men have to make to the ends of the world and back its the least they might get a squeeze or two at a woman while they can going out to be drowned or blown up somewhere I went up windmill hill to the flats that Sunday morning with Captain Rubios that was dead spyglass like the sentry had he said hed have one or two from on board I wore that frock from the B Marche Paris and the coral necklace the straits shining I could see over to Morocco almost the bay of Tangier white and the Atlas mountain with snow on it and the straits like a river so clear Harry Molly Darling I was thinking of him on the sea all the time after at mass when my petticoat began to slip down at the elevation weeks and weeks I kept the handkerchief under my pillow for the smell of him there was no decent perfume to be got in that Gibraltar only that cheap peau despagne that faded and left a stink on you more than anything else I wanted to give him a memento he gave me that clumsy Claddagh ring for luck that I gave Gardner going to South Africa where those Boers killed him with their war and fever but they were well beaten all the same as if it brought its bad luck with it like an opal or pearl must have been pure 16 carat gold because it was very heavy I can see his face clean shaven Frseeeeeeeeeeeeeeeeeefrong that train again weeping tone once in the dear deaead days beyond recall

Ulysses, pp. 903–4

The following extract describes yet another middle-ageing husband in the act of losing 'control' of his wife, not, by an act of determined will, nor like Bloom in *Ulysses* to an actual present lover. Gabriel Conroy in 'The Dead' (1906), after an evening of minor but telling *contretemps*, has been romanticising to himself his relationship to Gretta, his wife, as a kind of 'compensation'. It does not last.

36

He stood, holding her head between his hands. Then, slipping one arm swiftly about her body and drawing her towards him, he said softly:

67

'Gretta, dear, what are you thinking about?'

She did not answer nor yield wholly to his arm. He said again, softly:

'Tell me what it is, Gretta. I think I know what is the matter. Do I know?'

She did not answer at once. Then she said in an outburst of tears:

'O, I am thinking about that song, *The Lass of Aughrim*.'

She broke loose from him and ran to the bed and, throwing her arms across the bed-rail, hid her face. Gabriel stood stock-still for a moment in astonishment and then followed her. As he passed in the way of the cheval-glass he caught sight of himself in full length, his broad, well-filled shirt-front, the face whose expression always puzzled him when he saw it in a mirror and his glimmering gilt-rimmed eyeglasses. He halted a few paces from her and said:

'What about the song? Why does that make you cry?'

She raised her head from her arms and dried her eyes with the back of her hand like a child. A kinder note than he had intended went into his voice.

'Why, Gretta?' he asked.

'I am thinking about a person long ago who used to sing that song.'

'And who was the person long ago?' asked Gabriel, smiling.

'It was a person I used to know in Galway when I was living with my grandmother,' she said.

The smile passed away from Gabriel's face. A dull anger began to gather again at the back of his mind and the dull fires of his lust began to glow angrily in his veins.

'Someone you were in love with?' he asked ironically.

'It was a young boy I used to know,' she answered, 'named Michael Furey. He used to sing that song, *The Lass of Aughrim*. He was very delicate.'

Gabriel was silent. He did not wish her to think that he was interested in this delicate boy.

'I can see him so plainly,' she said, after a moment. 'Such eyes as he had: big dark eyes! And such an expression in them—an expression!'

'O then, you were in love with him?' said Gabriel.

'I used to go out walking with him,' she said, 'when I was in Galway.'

A thought flew across Gabriel's mind.

'Perhaps that was why you wanted to go to Galway with that Ivors girl?' he said coldly.

She looked at him and asked in surprise:

'What for?'

Her eyes made Gabriel feel awkward. He shrugged his shoulders and said:

'How do I know? To see him perhaps.'

She looked away from him along the shaft of light towards the window in silence.

'He is dead,' she said at length. 'He died when he was only seventeen. Isn't it a terrible thing to die so young as that?'

'What was he?' asked Gabriel, still ironically.

'He was in the gasworks,' she said.

Gabriel felt humiliated by the failure of his irony and by the evocation of this figure from the dead, a boy in the gasworks. While he had been full of memories of their secret life together, full of tenderness and joy and desire, she had been comparing him in her mind with another. A shameful consciousness of his own person assailed him. He saw himself as a ludicrous figure . . . a nervous well-meaning sentimentalist, orating to vulgarians and idealizing his own clownish lusts, the pitiable fatuous fellow he had caught a glimpse of in the mirror. Instinctively he turned his back more to the light lest she might see the shame that burned upon his forehead.

He tried to keep up his tone of cold interrogation, but his voice when he spoke was humble and indifferent.

'I suppose you were in love with this Michael Furey, Gretta,' he said.

'I was great with him at that time,' she said.

Her voice was veiled and sad. Gabriel, feeling now how vain it would be to try to lead her whither he had purposed, carressed one of her hands and said, also sadly :

'And what did he die of so young, Gretta? Consumption, was it?'

'I think he died for me,' she answered.

A vague terror seized Gabriel at this answer as if, at that hour when he had hoped to triumph, some impalpable and vindictive being was coming against him, gathering forces against him in its vague world. But he shook himself free of it with an effort of reason and continued to caress her hand. He did not question her again for he felt that she would tell him of herself. Her hand was warm and moist : it did not respond to his touch, but he continued to caress it just as he had caressed her first letter to him that spring morning. . . .

She was fast asleep.

Gabriel, leaning on his elbow, looked for a few moments unresentfully on her tangled hair and half-open mouth, listening to her deep-drawn breath. So she had had that romance in her life : a man had died for her sake. It hardly pained him now to think how poor a part he, her husband, had played in her life. He watched her while she slept as though he and she had never lived together as man and wife. His curious eyes rested long upon her face and on her hair : and, as he thought of what she must have been then, in that time of her first girlish beauty, a strange friendly pity for her entered his soul. He did not like to say even to himself that her face was no longer beautiful but he knew that it was no longer the face for which Michael Furey had braved death. . . .

The air of the room chilled his shoulders. He stretched himself cautiously along under the sheets and lay down beside his wife. One by one they were all becoming shades. Better pass boldly into that other world, in the full glory of some passion, than fade and wither dismally with age. He thought of how she who lay beside him had locked in her heart for so many years that image of her lover's eyes when he had told her that he did not wish to live.

Generous tears filled Gabriel's eyes. He had never felt that himself towards any woman but he knew that such a feeling must be love. The tears gathered more thickly in his eyes and in the partial darkness he imagined he saw the form of a young man standing under a dripping tree. Other forms were near. His soul had approached that region where dwell the vast hosts of the dead. He was conscious of, but could not apprehend, their wayward and flickering existence. His own identity was fading out into a grey impalpable world: the solid world itself, which these dead had one time reared and lived in was dissolving and dwindling.

A few light taps upon the pane made him turn to the window. It had begun to snow again. He watched sleepily the flakes, silver and dark, falling obliquely against the lamplight. The time had come for him to set out on his journey westward. Yes, the newspapers were right: snow was general all over Ireland. It was falling on every part of the dark central plain, on the treeless hills, falling softly upon the Bog of Allen and, farther westward, softly falling into the dark mutinous Shannon waves. It was falling, too, upon every part of the lonely churchyard on the hill where Michael Furey lay buried. It lay thickly drifted on the crooked crosses and headstones, on the spears of the little gate, on the barren thorns. His soul swooned slowly as he heard the snow falling faintly through the universe and faintly falling, like the descent of their last end, upon all the living and the dead.

Dubliners, pp. 510–14

Joyce surrounds his *finale* with ambiguity: is Gabriel overcoming his egotism, learning to accept his limited share of life, or is he giving up the fight, relaxing into a kind of living death? Or can both be true? This last story in *Dubliners*, written a few years after the others in the volume, turned out to be oddly prophetic of Joyce's concerns for the next fifteen years and more. Within a year of writing it, he was already planning *Ulysses*.

'Finnegans Wake'

For the next seventeen years, between bouts of iritis (an excruciatingly painful eye disease), Joyce worked at a book which came to be called his 'Work in Progress'. Its final title, *Finnegans Wake*, only became generally known with its publication in 1939.

After Joyce completed *Ulysses* he was asked what he was going to write next and he replied, 'a history of the world', which is what *Finnegans Wake* is: an allegorical history of the universe, from creation to judgement day. Like Jonathan Swift's *A Tale of a Tub* (which Joyce often alludes to), the *Wake* presents its essentially comic version of history in the guise of events happening to particular individuals. But where in Swift, Peter, Martin and Jack stand for Roman Catholicism, Lutheranism (and later the Church of England) and Calvinism, Joyce's characters stand for no particular institutions, but rather for general forces and impulses and 'principles' underlying universal history. Often the events in Joyce's homely domestic plot —which concerns a Dublin publican, Humphrey Chimpden Earwicker (HCE) and his family—are made to stand simutaneously for a *number* of historical events. Joyce effects this by *punning*.

For example: one of Earwicker's sons is the 'artist-type'
of person, very like James Joyce himself. (The Earwicker
family story is often an allegory of the Joyce family.) One
of the questions asked this artist is, 'Was liffe worth
leaving?' This means both 'Was life worth living' and
'Was Liffey worth leaving?' The River Liffey runs through
Dublin and so the second question means, was it worth it
for the artist to leave Dublin (and go to live on the Continent). A little later, the same questioner says,

37

But, by Jove Chronides, Seed of Summ, after at he had
bate his breastplates for, forforget, forforgetting his birds-
place, it was soon that, that he, that he rehad himself.
By a prayer? No, that comes later. By contrite attrition?
Nay, that we passed. Mid esercizism? So is nicht.

Finnegans Wake, p. 231

This is an explanation of how the Artist regained his self-
confidence (rehad himself), which he had lost (as did
Stephen Dedalus) sometime after his first 'leaving' of
Dublin. The stuttering of the speaker here (for, forforget,
forforgetting . . . that, that he, that he rehad), the reader
of *Finnegans Wake* comes to recognise as the trait of
the artist's brother, who is in every way his polar opposite,
and so we must be wary of the 'explanation' offered. That
explanation is obscure, no doubt deliberately, for such
things are very difficult to explain. The Artist rehad himself
'Mid esercizism', says the speaker, and it is the reader's job
to sort out the real words which have gone to make up
this phrase: Mid is short for *amid*, but it is also the way
a German pronounces *mitt* (which means *with*). 'Esercizism' is harder, perhaps finally impenetrable though con-

74

tinually teasing: it appears to contain parts of the words
exorcism, exercise, esoteric. All these and others (*essor*
is a root stem meaning *flight*) are serio-comic explanations
of the regaining of self-confidence which should have
obvious significance for the reader familiar with Joyce's
own life and writing. But at the same time as the real
reason is held out to us it is shrouded in even darker
mystery. Some readers will think this kind of thing very
funny; others will not, and they will never think much
of *Finnegans Wake*.

Joyce calls his book,

a grand funferall
this sound seemetery
this claybook
this allaphbed
the meandertale *and* a meanderthalltale
the book of Doublends Jined
this Eyrawyggla saga
the humphriad
a puling sample jungle of woods
this oldworld epistola
the gobbleydumped turkery
this prepronomial funferall
the Tiberiast duplex
Miliken's Make
your new Irish stew
the Wake

These are only a few of what the names for the *Wake*
itself, all taken from the first two hundred pages, and the
actual title is not used until page 607. In addition to
hundreds of others, similar phrases refer to the book at
second hand: that is, they describe its hero or a mysterious
letter supposed to have been dictated by his wife to his
artist son. The letter is an attempt to exonerate the hero

from certain accusations made against him, and so, in a manner of speaking the letter is a symbol for Joyce's book as a whole. The letter is called at one point 'this radio-ossilating epiepistle', a description which fits *Finnegans Wake* itself, oscillating like radio waves (perhaps between the Dublin Earwickers and all of history) and if not a full-fledged 'epistle' (as say, the Bible is complete from Genesis to Apocalypse then at least an 'epiepistle', a letter 'based on' (*epi*) a larger epistle, as an *epicycle* is a small circle revolving on the circumference of a larger one.

In the first chapter we read of the death of Finnegan[1]—he falls off his ladder—and of his wake. The hod-carrier is here a symbol for the mythic Irish hero Finn (and both are further associated with many other heroic figures of the past). When Finnegan (or Finn) sits up at his wake, the mourners ask him to lie down again and play dead: 'Aisy now, you decent man, with your knees and lie quiet and repose your honour's lordship!' The heroic age is over and the great Finn's modern replacement, domestic, bourgeois Earwicker's story begins.

A plot outline begins to form and we are introduced to Earwicker, his ancestry, how he got his name, *etc*. As is usual in *Finnegans Wake*, there are many alternative explantations presented for each 'fact', and even different facts are put forward, with varying (and usually mutually contradictory) authority.

Among many other humorous confusions about Earwicker is the extremely important one of the 'alleged misdemeanour'. At first, without giving us *the facts*, our author is inclined to take Earwicker's side.

---

[1] The original 'Finnegans Wake' is a ballad about a hod-carrier who sits up in his coffin when a mourner inadvertently pours whisky over him.

38

Slander, let it lie its flattest, has never been able to convict
our good and great and no ordinary Southron Earwicker,
that homogenius man, as pious author called him, of any
graver impropriety than that . . . of having behaved with
ongentilmensky immodus opposite a pair of dainty maidservants in the swoolth of the rushy hollow whither, or
so the two gown and pinners pleaded, dame nature in all
innocency had spontaneously and about the same hour of
the eventide sent them both.

Finnegans Wake, p. 34

This seem to imply that Earwicker had exposed himself
to the two 'dainty maidservants', but our 'pious author'
immediately casts doubt on their 'testimonies' and attempts
to excuse his hero: 'a first offence . . . with such attenuat-
ing circumstances . . . an abnormal Saint Swithin's summer
and . . . a ripe occasion to provoke it.'

On the other hand there is little doubt that Earwicker
acts guiltily. One day 'ages and ages after the alleged
misdemeanour' he is asked the time of day by 'a cad
with a pipe', and instead of a normal answer, Earwicker
defends himself at immense length ('there is not one little
of truth, allow me to tell you, in that purest of fibfib fab-
rications'—like the son who takes after him, Earwicker is a
stutterer).

But rumour gets around, and a ballad is even made up on
the subject of the hero, 'The Ballad of Persse O'Reilly'.
(Persse O'Reilly is Earwicker. Earwicker is often punned
with 'earwig', which in French is *perce oreille*.)

Joyce arranges an extravagant trial for Earwicker, with
many accusers and much cross-evidence presented. Eventually we come to his wife's defence, the letter mentioned

before, but by this time the matter has become so obscure that the narrator becomes a kind of professor of philology, who attempts to explain the letter as though it were one of the great mysteries of the world. (Here also *Finnegans Wake* is like *A Tale of a Tub*, which has many digressions equally intended as satires on the learned world.) This explanation only complicates things further, and the joke comes to be on the 'explainers' of this world.

When we finally get back to the Earwickers, it begins to look like much, if not all of what we have been reading, is really Humphrey's *dream*—the pattern of glorification and accusation is similar to Bloom's treatment in the surrealist fantasy of the brothel chapter in *Ulysses*. The latter part of the *Wake* seems to carry us through to morning and many phrases suggest that in the world-history allegory morning is Resurrection Day ('Array! Surrection. Eireweeker to the wohld bludyn world. O rally, O rally, O rally!'). There has been much debate over just who is the dreamer in *Finnegans Wake*. Humphrey has been objected to, as not likely to have in his head all the miscellaneous and esoteric knowledge with which the book is packed. But that is not really a proper objection. The *Wake* can be Humphrey's dream, or James Joyce's dream or the Dream of Mankind or life itself, perhaps the greatest dream of all. In *Finnegans Wake* none of the characters is an 'individual'; they are all *composites*, like photographic prints made from a number of superimposed negatives,

39

Whence it is a slopperish matter, given the wet and low visibility (since in this scherzarade of one's thousand one nightinesses that sword of certainty which would

indentifide the body never falls) to idendifine the individ-
uone. . . .

Finnegans Wake, p. 51

First the Fall of Finnegan and the lamentation (and celebration) at his wake.

40

What then agentlike brought about that tragoady thun-
dersday this municipal sin business? . . . . Heed! Heed!
It may half been a missfired brick, as some say, or it mought
have been due to a collupsus of his back promises, as others
looked at it. (There extand by now one thousand and one
stories, all told, of the same). . . .

His howd feeled heavy, his hoddit did shake. (There was
a wall of course in erection) Dimb! He stottered from
the latter. Damb! he was dud. Dumb! Mastabatoom, mas-
tabadtomm, when a mon merries his lute is all long. For
whole the world to see.

Shize? I should shee! Macool, Macool, orra whyi deed ye
diie? of a trying thirstay mournin? Sobs they sighdid at
Fillagain's chrissormiss wake, all the hoolivans of the
nation, prostrated in their consternation and their duodisi-
mally profusive plethora of ululation. There was plumbs
and grumes and cheriffs and citherers and raiders and cine-
men too. And the all gianed in with the shoutmost shovia-
lity. Agog and magog and the round of them agrog. To the
continuation of that celebration until Hanandhunigan's
extermination! Some in kinkin corass, more, kankan keen-
ing. Belling him up and filling him down. He's stiff but
he's steady is Priam Olim! 'Twas he was the dacent gay-
labouring youth. Sharpen his pillowscone, tap up his bier!
E'erawhere in this whorl would ye hear sich a din again?
With their deepbrow fundigs and the dusty fidelios. They
laid him brawdawn alanglast bed. With a bockalips of
finisky fore his feet. And a barrowload of guenesis hoer his

head. Tee the tootal of the fluid hang the twoddle of the fuddled, O!

Finnegans Wake, pp. 5–6

The whisky (usquebagh) wakes Tim Finnegan up, but the mourners ask him to remain dead. Healiopolis is Dublin, renamed for the politician Tim Healey. Reasons are advanced why Finnegan is better off dead and with the heroes of the past (Brian Boru, Genghis Khan, *etc.*). Moreover, they'll look after his grave.

41

Usqueadbaugham! Anam muck an dhoul! Did ye drink me doornail?

Now be aisy, good Mr Finnimore, sir. And take your laysure like a god on pension and don't be walking abroad. Sure you'd only lose yourself in Healiopolis. . . . Meeting some sick old bankrupt or the Cotterick's donkey with his shoe hanging, clankatachankata, or a slut snoring with an impure infant on a bench. 'Twould turn you against life, so 'twould. And the weather's that mean too. . . . You're better off, sir, where you are, primesigned in the full of your dress, bloodeagle waistcoat and all, remembering your shapes and sizes on the pillow of your baby-curls under your sycamore by the keld water where the Tory's clay will scare the varmints and have all you want, pouch, gloves, flask, bricket, kerchief, ring and amberulla, the whole treasure of the pyre, in the land of souls with Homin and Broin Baroke and pole ole Lonan and Nobucketnozzler and the Guinnghis Khan. And we'll be coming here, the ombre players, to rake your gravel and bringing you presents, won't we, fenians? And it isn't our spittle we'll stint you of, is it, druids? Not shabbty little imagettes, pennydirts and dodgemyeyes you buy in the soottee stores. But offerings of the field.

Finnegans Wake, p. 24

'Already' Finn (Mr. Finnimore) has been replaced (Finn-no-more) by Humphrey Chimpden Earwicker ('*H*umme the *C*heapner, *E*sc'), ' a big rody ram lad'. He is the height of a *chimney* and he *humphs* and he has 'a pocked wife' and three children, two boys and a girl.

42

Repose you now! Finn no more!

For, be that samesake sibsubstitute of a hooky salmon, there's already a big rody ram lad at random on the premises of his haunt of the hungred bordles, as it is told me. Shop Illicit, flourishing like a lordmajor or a buaboabaybohm, litting flop a deadlop (aloose!) to lee but lifting a bennbranch a yardalong (ivoeh!) on the breezy side (for showm!), the height of Brewster's chimpney and as broad below as Phineas Barnum; humphing his share of the showthers is senken on him he's such a grandfallar, with a pocked wife in pickle that's a flyfire and three lice nittle clinkers, two twilling bugs and one midgit pucelle. And aither he cursed and recursed and was everseen doing what your fourfootlers saw or he was never done seeing what you cool-pigeons know, weep the clouds aboon for smile-down witnesses, and that'll do now about the fairyhees and the frailysshees. . . . But however 'twas 'tis sure for one thing, what sherif Toragh voucherfors and Mapqiq makes put out, that the man, Humme the Cheapner, Esc, overseen as we thought him, yet a worthy of the the naym, came at this timecoloured place where we live in our paroqial fermament one tide on another. . . .

Finnegans Wake, p. 29

'Cursed and recursed' puns of the *corso* and *recorso*, the cycle of history in the philosophy of Giambattista Vico (1668 1744), a jurist and professor of 'eloquence' at the University of Naples. (See Books I and IV of his *The New Science*.)

We see here a capsule version of Earwicker's 'alleged misdemeanour': HCE, in the course of his Dublin life, was seen 'doing what your fourfootlers saw'. (The 'fourfootlers' are his four principal accusers, sometimes the four gospellers and the Four Masters, authors of a famous Irish history, as well.) Whatever the truth, HCE 'came at this timecoloured place' to Ireland.

A lengthy story is told of how Earwicker got his odd surname—supposedly conferred for a remark he made about earwigs by an 'ancient' king who has the 'walrus moustaches' of Edward VII but is also called 'Our sailor king'. Immediately, however, three other versions of the story are suggested, which eventually lead us to the story of the misdemeanour.

43

A baser meaning has been read into these characters the literal sense of which decency can safely scarcely hint. It has been blurtingly bruited by certain wisecrackers (the stinks of Mohorat are in the nightplots of the morning), that he suffered from a vile disease. Athma, unmanner them! To such a suggestion the one selfrespecting answer is to affirm that there are certain statements which ought not to be, and one should like to hope to be able to add, ought not to be allowed to be made. Nor have his detractors, who, an imperfectly warmblooded race, apparently conceive him as a great white caterpillar capable of any and every enormity in the calendar recorded to the discredit of the Juke and Kellikek families, mended their case by insinuating that, alternately, he lay at one time under the ludicrous imputation of annoying Welsh fusiliers in the people's park. Hay, hay, hay! Hoq, hoq, hoq! Faun and Flora on the lea love that little old joq. To anyone who knew and loved the christlikeness of the big cleanminded giant H. C. Earwicker throughout his

excellency long vicefreegal existence the mere suggestion
of him as a lustsleuth nosing for trouble in a boobytrap
rings particularly preposterous. Truth, beard on prophet,
compels one to add that there is said to have been quon-
dam (pfuit! pfuit!) some case of the kind implicating,
it is interdum believed, a quidam (if he did not exist it
would be necessary quoniam to invent him) abhout that
time stambuling haround Dumbaling in leaky sneakers. . . .

Finnegans Wake, p. 33

The Jukes and the Kallikaks were American hillbilly
families whose histories were said to prove the degeneracy
resulting from consanguineous marriages.

The rumours ('unfacts') about Humphrey will not hold
up under legal scrutiny. Nevertheless there is something
odd about the portrait of him in the National Gallery.
And there *was* a trial.

44

Thus the unfacts, did we possess them, are too imprecisely
few to warrant our certitude, the evidencegivers by legpoll
too untrustworthy irreperible where his adjugers are
semmingly freak threes but his judicandees plainly minus
twos. Nevertheless Madam's Toshowus waxes largely more
lifeliked (entrance, one kudos; exits, free) and our notional
gullery is now completely complacent, an exegious monu-
ment, aerily perennious. Oblige with your blackthorns;
gamps, degrace! And there many have paused before that
exposure of him by old Tom Quad, a flashback in which
he sits sated, gowndabout, in clericalease habit, watching
bland sol slithe dodgsomely into the nethermore, a globule
of maugdleness about to corrugitate his mild dewed cheek
and the tata of a tiny victorienne, Alys, pressed by his
limper looser.

Yet certes one is. Eher the following winter had overed
the pages of nature's book and till Ceadurbar-atta-Cleath

became Dablena Tertia, the shadow of the huge outlander, maladik, multvult, magnoperous, had bulked at the bar of a rota of tribunals in manor hall as in thieves' kitchen, mid pillow talk and chithouse chat, on Marlborough Green as through Molesworth Fields, here sentenced pro tried with Jedburgh justice, there acquitted contestimony with benefit of clergy. His Thing Mod have undone him : and his madthing has done him man. His beneficiaries are legion in the part he created : they number up his years. Great-wheel Dunlop was the name was on him : behung, all we are his bisaacles. As hollyday in his house so was he priest and king to that : ulvy came, envy saw, ivy conquered. Lou! Lou! They have waved his green boughs o'er him as they have torn him limb from lamb.

Finnegans Wake, p. 57

Ritually 'torn limb from lamb', HCE is here a kind of Orpheus and also like Christ, the Lamb of God.

Dozens of witnesses appear, giving much contradictory testimony. Eventually one of HCE's sons is charged as well—a new trial which, dream-like, merges with the father's trial—and we begin to meet the younger generation.

45

. . . little headway, if any, was made in solving the wasnottobe crime cunundrum when a child of Maam, Festy King, of a family long and honourably associated with the tar and feather industries, who gave an address in old plomansch Mayo of the Saxons in the heart of a foulfamed potheen district, was subsequently haled up at the Old Bailey on the calends of Mars, under an incompatibly framed indictment of both the counts (from each equinoxious points of view, the one fellow's fetch being the other fellow's person) that is to see, flying cushats out of his ouveralls and making fesses immodst his forces on the

field. Oyeh! Oyeh! When the prisoner, soaked in methyl-
ated, appeared in dry dock, appatently ambrosiaenculised,
like Kersse's Korduroy Karikature, wearing, besides stains,
rents and patches, his fight shirt, straw braces, souwester
and a policeman's corkscrew trowswers, all out of the
true (as he has purposely torn up all his cymtrymanx
bespokes in the mamertime), deposing for his exution with
all the fluors of sparse in the royal Irish vocabulary
how the whole padderjagmartin tripiezite suet and all the
sulfeit of copperas had fallen off him quatz unaccountably
like the chrystalisations of Alum on Even while he was
trying for to stick fire to himcell, (in feacht he was dripping
as he found upon stripping for a pipkin ofmalt as he
feared the coold raine) it was attempted by the crown
(P.C. Robort) to show that King, *elois* Crowbar, once
known as Meleky, impersonating a climbing boy, rubbed
some pixes of any luvial peatsmoor o'er his face, plucks
and pussas, with a clanetourf as the best means of dis-
guising himself and was to the middlewhite fair in Mud-
ford of a Thoorsday, feishts of Peeler and Pole, under the
illassumed names of Tykingfest and Rabworc picked by
him and Anthony out of a tellafun book, ellegedly with
a pedigree pig (unlicensed) and a hyacinth.

Finnegans Wake, pp. 85–6

The accused at *this* trial is Shem ('short for Seumas'),
the Artist. Here his brother Shaun appears for the first
time as the accuser. Eventually whole chapters are given
over to Shaun's accusations.

46

Remarkable evidence was given, anon, by an eye, ear,
nose and throat witness, whom Wesleyan chapelgoers sus-
pected of being a plain clothes priest W.P., situate at Null-
null, Medical Square, who, upon letting down his rice
and peacegreen coverdisk and having been sullenly cau-

tioned against yawning while being grilled, smiled (he had
had a onebumper at parting from Mrs Molroe in the morning) and stated to his eliciter under his morse mustaccents
(gobbless!) that he slept with a bonafides and that he
would be there to remember the filth of November, hatinar-
ing, rowdy O, which, with the jiboulees of Juno and the
dates of ould lanxiety, was going, please the Rainmaker,
to decembs within the ephemerides of profane history, all
one with Tournay, Yetstoslay and Temorah.

Finnegans Wake, pp. 86–7

At the end of HCE's trial we hear of 'the letter', and
'the four'—the trial judges—discuss over and over what
has happened, always returning to gossip about Humphrey,
'the great Howdoyoucallem'.

47

And so it all ended. Artha kama dharma moksa.[2] Ask
Kavya[3] for the kay. And so everybody heard their plaint
and all listened to their plause. The letter! The litter!
And the soother the bitther! Of eyebrow pencilled, by
lipstipple penned. Borrowing a word and begging the
question and stealing tinder and slipping like soap. . . .
The solid man saved by his sillied woman. Crackajolking
away like a hearse on fire. The elm that whimpers at the
top told the stone that moans when stricken. Wind broke
it. Wave bore it. Reed wrote of it. Syce ran with it. Hand
tore it and wild went war. Hen trieved it and plight
pledged peace. It was folded with cunning, sealed with
crime, uptied by a harlot, undone by a child. It was life
but was it fair? It was free but was it art? The old hunks
on the hill read it to perlection. It made ma make merry
and sissy so shy and rubbed some shine off Shem and put
some shame into Shaun. . . . So there you are now there

[2] Success, pleasure, duty, enlightenment: the four Hindu 'ends
of life'.
[3] The poet (Hindu).

they were, when all was over again, the four with them,
setting around upin their judges' chambers, in the muni-
ment room, of their marshalsea, under the suspices of
Lally, around their old traditional tables of the law like
Somany Solans to talk it over rallthesameagain. Well and
druly dry. Suffering law the dring. Accourting to king's
evelyns. So help her goat and kiss the bouc. Festives and
highajinks and jintyaun and her beetyrossy bettydoaty
and not to forget now a'duna o'darnel. The four of them
and thank court now there were no more of them. So
pass the push for port sake. Be it soon. Ah ho! And do
you remember, Singabob, the badfather, the same, the
great Howdoyoucallem, and his old nickname, Dirty
Daddy Pantaloons, in his monopoleums. . . . And so they
went on, the fourbottle men, the analists, unguam and
nunguam and lunguam again, their anschluss about her
whosebefore and his whereafters and how she was lost
away away in the fern and how he was founded deap on
deep in anear, and the rustlings and the twitterings and
the raspings and the snappings and the sighings and the
paintings and the ukukuings and the (hist!) the springa-
partings and the (hast!) the bybyscuttlings and all the
scandalmunkers and the pure craigs that used to be (up)
that time living and lying and rating and riding round
Nunsbelly Square.

Finnegans Wake, pp. 93–5

Interest transfers to the Letter and its author, Earwicker's wife, usually called some variant of 'Anna Livia
Plurabelle'—as Ann, Anna, ALP. The narrator metamor-
phoses into a philologist, who decides, among much else,
that the letter was scratched up by a hen (Belinda Doran),
herself a version of ALP

48

Closer inspection of the *bordereau* would reveal a multiplicity of personalities inflicted on the documents or document and some prevision of virtual crime or crimes might be made by anyone unwary enough before any suitable occasion for it or them had so far managed to happen along. In fact, under the closed eyes of the inspectors the traits featuring the *chiaroscuro* coalesce their contrarieties eliminated, in one stable somebody. . . .

Say, baroun lousadoor, who in hallhagal wrote the durn thing anyhow? Erect, beseated, mountback, against a partywall, below freezigrade, by the use of quill or style, with turbid or pellucid mind, accompanied or the reverse by mastication, interrupted by visit of seer to scribe or of scribe to site, atwixt two showers or atosst of a trike, rained upon or blown around, by a rightdown regular racer from the soil or by a too pained whittlewit laden with the loot of learning?

Now, patience; and remember patience is the great thing, and above all things else we must avoid anything like being or becoming out of patience. A good plan used by worried business folk who may not have had many momentums to master Kung's doctrine of the meang or the propriety codestruces of Carprimustimus is just to think of all the sinking fund of patience possessed in their conjoint names by both brothers Bruce. . . .

Naysayers we know. To conclude purely negatively from the positive absence of political odia and monetary requests that its page cannot ever have been a penproduct of a man or woman of that period or those parts is only one more unlookedfor conclusion leaped at, being tantamount to inferring from the nonpresence of inverted commas (sometimes called quotation marks) on any page that its author was always constitutionally incapable of misappropriating the spoken words of others.

. . . to concentrate solely on the literal sense or even the psychological content of any document to the sore neglect of the enveloping facts themselves circumstan-
88

tiating it is just as hurtful to sound sense (and let it be added to the truest taste). . . .

> [*It is notable how few punning neologisms there are in this section.*]

The bird in the case was Belinda of the Dorans, a more than quinquegintarian (Terziis prize with Serni medal, Cheepalizzy's Hane Exposition) and what she was scratching at the hour of klokking twelve looked for all this zogzag world like a goodish-sized sheet of letterpaper originating by transhipt from Boston (Mass.) of the last of the first to Dear whom it proceded to mention Maggy well & allathome's health well only the hate turned the mild on *the van* Houtens and the general's elections with a *lovely* face of some born gentleman with a beautiful present of wedding cakes for dear thankyou Chriesty and with grand funferall of poor Father Michael don't forget unto life's & Muggy well how are you Maggy & hopes soon to hear well & must now close it with fondest to the twoinns with four crosskisses for holy paul holey corner holipoli whollyisland pee ess from (locust may eat all but this sign shall they never) affectionate largelooking tache of tch. The stain, and that a teastain (the overcautelousness of the masterbilker here, as usual, signing the page away), marked it off on the spout of the moment as a genuine relique of ancient Irish pleasant pottery of that lydialike languishing class known as a hurry-me-o'er-the-hazy.

Why then how?

Well, almost any photoist worth his chemicots will tip anyone asking him the teaser that if a negative of a horse happens to melt enough while drying, well, what you do get is, well, a positively grotesquely distorted macromass of all sorts of horsehappy values and masses of meltwhile horse. Tip. Well, this freely is what must have occurred to our missive (there's a sod of a turb for you! please wisp off the grass!) unfilthed from the boucher by

the sagacity of a lookmelittle likemelong hen. Heated
residence in the heart of the orangeflavoured mudmound
had partly obliterated the negative to start with, causing
some features palpably nearer your pecker to be swollen
up most grossly while the farther back we manage to
wiggle the more we need the loan of a lens to see as much
as the hen saw.

Finnegans Wake, pp. 107–8 and pp. 111–2

The analysis of the Letter blossoms into a full-fledged
lecture in the form of a dozen questions and answers. The
narrator has become a Shaun-character, a sober, stick-in-
the-mud citizen, who devotes an entire chapter to reviling
his brother Shem, often recognisable as Joyce himself.

49

Shem is as short for Shemus as Jem is joky for Jacob. A
few toughnecks are still getatable who pretend that abori-
ginally he was of respectable stemming (he was an outlex
between the lines of Ragonar Blaubarb and Horrild Hair-
wire and an inlaw to Capt. the Hon. and Rev. Mr
Bbyrdwood de Trop Blogg was among his most distant
connections) but every honest to goodness man in the land
of the space of today knows that his back life will not
stand being written about in black and white. Putting truth
and untruth together a shot may be made at what this
hybrid actually was like to look at.

Shem's bodily getup, it seems, included an adze of a
skull, an eight of a larkseye, the whoel of a nose, one numb
arm up a sleeve, fortytwo hairs off his uncrown, eighteen
to his mock lip, a trio of barbels from his megageg chin
(sowman's son), the wrong shoulder higher than the right,
all ears, an artificial tongue with a natural curl, not a
foot to stand on, a handful of thumbs, a blind stomach, a
deaf heart, a loose liver, two fifths of two buttocks, one
gleetsteen avoirdupoider for him, a manroot of all evil, a

salmonkelt's thinskin, eelsblood in his cold toes, a bladder tristended. . . .

Rosbif of Old Zealand! he could not attouch it. See what happens when your somatophage merman takes his fancy to our virgitarian swan? He even ran away with hunself and became a farsoonerite, saying he would far sooner muddle through the hash of lentils in Europe than meddle with Irrland's split little pea. Once when among those rebels in a state of hopelessly helpless intoxication the piscivore strove to lift a czitround peel to either nostril, hiccuping, apparently impromptued by the hibat he had with his glottal stop, that he kukkakould flowrish for ever by the smell, as the czitr, as the kcedron, like a scedar, of the founts, on mountains, with limon on, of Lebanon. O! the lowness of him was beneath all up to that sunk to! No likedbylike firewater of firstserved firstshot or gulletburn gin or honest brewbarrett beer either. O dear no! Instead the tragic jester sobbed himself wheywhingingly sick of life on some sort of a rhubarbarous maundarin yellagreen funkleblue windigut diodying applejack squeezed from sour grapefruice. . . . You see, chaps, it will trickle out, freaksily of course, but the tom and the shorty of it is: he was in his bardic memory low. All the time he kept on treasuring with condign satisfaction each and every crumb of trektalk, covetous of his neighbour's word, and if ever, during a Munda conversazione commoted in the nation's interest, delicate tippits were thrown out to him touching his evil courses by some wellwishers, vainly pleading by scriptural arguments with the opprobrious papist about trying to brace up for the kidos of the thing, Scally wag, and be a men instead of a dem scrounger, dish it all . . . without one sigh of haste like the supreme prig he was, and not a bit sorry, he would pull a vacant landlubber's face . . . and begin to tell all the intelligentsia admitted to that tamileasy samtalaisy conclamazzione . . . the whole lifelong swrine story of his entire low cornaille existence, abusing his

deceased ancestors wherever the sods were and one
moment tarabooming great blunderguns (poh!) about his
farfamed fine Poppamore, Mr Humhum, whom history,
climate and entertainment made the first of his sept and
always up to debt, though Eavens ears ow many fines
he faces, and another moment visanvrerssas, cruaching
three jeers (pah!) for his rotten little ghost of a Peppybeg,
Mr Himmyshimmy, a blighty, a reeky, a lighty, a scrapy,
a babbly, a ninny, dirty seventh among thieves and always
bottom sawyer, till nowan knowed how howmely howme
could be, giving unsolicited testimony on behalf of the
absent, as glib as eaveswater to those present (who mean-
while, with increasing lack of interest in his semantics,
allowed various subconscious smickers to drivel slowly
across their fichers), unconsciously explaining, for ink-
stands, with a meticulosity bordering on the insane, the
various meanings of all the different foreign parts of speech
he misused . . . [H]e had flickered up and flinnered down
into a drug and drunkery addict, growing megalomane
of a loose past. This explains the litany of septuncial
lettertrumpets honorific, highpitched, erudite, neo-
classical, which he so loved as patricianly to manuscribe
after his name. It would have diverted, if ever seen, the
shuddersome spectacle of this semidemented zany amid
the inspissated grime of his glaucous den making believe
to read his usylessly unreadable Blue Book of Eccles,
édition de ténèbres, (even yet sighs the Most Different,
Dr Poindejenk, authorised bowdler and censor, it can't be
repeated!) turning over three sheets at a wind, telling
himself delightedly, no espellor mor so, that every splurge
on the vellum he blundered over was an aisling vision
more gorgeous than the one before. . . .

Finnegans Wake, pp. 169-79

The 'usylessly unreadable Blue Book of Eccles'? *Ulysses*,
of course, written by that Shem-figure James Joyce.

A chapter is given over to the Mother. It is spoken by

two old women washing the Earwicker laundry on the banks of the Liffey, which flows through Dublin. They gossip about the family.

50

O

tell me all about
Anna Livia! I want to hear all
about Anna Livia. Well, you know Anna Livia? Yes, of course, we all know Anna Livia. Tell me all. Tell me now. You'll die when you hear. Well, you know, when the old cheb went futt and did what you know. Yes, I know, go on. Wash quit and don't be dabbling. Tuck up your sleeves and loosen your talktapes. And don't butt me—hike!— when you bend. Or whatever it was they threed to make out he thried to two in the Fiendish park. He's an awful old reppe. Look at the shirt of him! Look at the dirt of it! He has all my water black on me. And it steeping and stuping since this time last wik. How many goes is it I wonder I washed it? I know by heart the places he likes to saale, duddurty devil! Scorching my hand and starving my famine to make his private linen public. Wallop it well with your battle and clean it. My wrists are wrusty rubbing the mouldaw stains. And the dneepers of wet and the gangres of sin in it! What was it he did a tail at all on Animal Sendai? And how long was he under loch and neagh? It was put in the newses what he did, nicies and priers, the King fierceas Humphrey, with illysus dis- tilling, exploits and all. But toms will till. I know he well. Temp untamed will hist for no man. As you spring so shall you neap.

Finnegans Wake, p. 196

This chapter has the names of hundreds of riverswoven into it (here the Moldau, Dneiper, Ganges and what others?). Mother Anna Livia Plurabelle—whose own name enshrines the Liffey—is the river itself in the 'nature allegory' of the *Wake*.

Working backwards in time, they speak of Anna's children and then Anna herself in the days before her marriage.

51

Onon! Onon! tell me more. Tell me every tiny teign. I want to know every single ingul. Down to what made the potters fly into jagsthole. And why were the vesles vet. That homa fever's winning me wome. If a mahun of the horse but hard me! We'd be bundukiboi meet askarigal. Well, now comes the hazel-hatchery part. After Clondalkin the King's Inns. We'll soon be there with the freshet. How many aleveens had she in tool? I can't rightly rede you that. Close only knows. Some say she had three figures to fill and confined herself to a hundred eleven, wan bywan bywan, making meanacuminamoyas. Olaph lamm et, all that pack? We won't have room in the kirkeyaard. She can't remember half the cradlenames she smacked on them by the grace of her boxing bishop's infallible slipper, the cane for Kund and abbles for Eyolf and ayther nayther for Yakov Yea. A hundred and how? They did well to rechristen her Pluhurabelle. O loreley! What a loddon lodes! Heigh ho! But it's quite on the cards she'll shed more and merrier, twills and trills, sparefours and spoilfives, nordsihkes and sudsevers and ayes and neins to a litter. Grandfarthring nap and Messamisery and the knave of all knaves and the joker. Heehaw! She must have been a gadabount in her day, so she must, more than most. Shoal she was, gidgad. She had a flewmen of her owen. Then a toss nare scared that lass, so aimai moe, that's agapo! Tell me, tell me, how cam she camlin through all her fellows, the neckar she was, the diveline? Casting her perils before our swains from Fonte-in-Monte to Tidingtown and from Tidingtown tilhavet. Linking one and knocking the next, tapting a flank and tipting a jutty and palling in and pietaring out and clyding by on her eastway.

Finnegans Wake, pp. 201–2

Anna 'making up'.

52

First she let her hair fal and down it flussed to her feet its teviots winding coils. Then, mothernaked, she sampood herself with galawater and fraguant pistania mud, wupper and lauar, from crown to sole. Next she greesed the groove of her keel, warthes and wears and mole and itcher, with antifouling butterscatch and turfentide and serpenthyme and with leafmould she ushered round prunella isles and eslats dun, quincecunct, allover her little mary. Peeld gold of waxwork her jellybelly and her grains of incense anguille bronze. And after that she wove a garland for her hair. She pleated it. She plaited it. Of meadowgrass and riverflags, the bulrush and waterweed, and of fallen griefs of weeping willow. Then she made her bracelets and her anklets and her armlets and a jetty amulet for necklace of clicking cobbles and pattering pebbles and rumbledown rubble, richmond and rehr, of Irish rhunerhinerstones and shellmarble bangles. That done, a dawk of smut to her airy ey, Annushka Lutetiavitch Pufflovah, and the lellipos cream to her lippeleens and the pick of the paintbox for her pommettes, from strawbirry reds to extra violates, and she sendred her boudeloire maids to His Affluence, Ciliegia Grande and Kirschie Real, the two chirsines, with respecks from his missus, seepy and sewery, and a request might she passe of him for a minnikin. A call to pay and light a taper, in Brie-on-Arrosa, back in a sprizzling. The cock striking mine, the stalls bridely sign, there's Zambosy waiting for Me! She said she wouldn't be half her length away. Then,

then, as soon as the lump his back was turned, with her mealiebag slang over her shulder, Anna Livia, oysterface, forth of her bassein came.

Finnegans Wake, pp. 206–7

Joyce was especially proud of his achievement in this chapter, particularly for its rhythms and sound. Indeed he claimed the whole book would make immediate sense to anyone who heard it read aloud! When a recording was made of Joyce reading a portion of *Finnegans Wake*, he chose to read the last pages of this chapter, ending with the following words. (The old women are slowly turning into a tree and a stone by the river's side as they gossip about Anna.)

53

Can't hear with the waters of. The chittering waters of. Flittering bats, fieldmice bawk talk. Ho! Are you not gone ahome? What Thom Malone? Can't hear with bawk of bats, all thim liffeying waters of. Ho, talk save us! My foos won't moos. I feel as old as yonder elm. A tale told of Shaun or Shem? All Livia's daughtersons. Dark hawks hear us. Night! Night! My ho head halls. I feel as heavy as yonder stone. Tell me of John or Shaun? Who were Shem and Shaun the living sons or daughters of? Night now! Tell me, tell me, tell me, elm! Night night! Telmetale of stem or stone. Beside the rivering waters of, hitherandthithering waters of. Night!

Finnegans Wake, pp. 215–6

The following chapters are given over to the children. The first is taken up with their games and with an improvised play they perform, titled 'The Mime of Mick [St. Michael], Nick [the Devil] and the Maggies'. Shaun, of course, plays the good St. Michael and Shem, the wicked Devil. The 'Mime', whose 'playbill' Joyce gives us, is yet another version of the Earwicker family history, and the rivalry of the brothers for the favour of their sister Issy comes to the fore.

54

Every evening at lighting up o'clock sharp and until further notice in Feenichts Playhouse. (Bar and conveniences always open, Diddlem Club douncestears.) Entrancings: gads, a scrab; the quality, one large shilling. Newly billed for each wickeday perfumance. Somndoze massinees. By arraignment, childream's hours, expercatered. Jampots, rinsed porters, taken in token. With nightly redistribution of parts and players by the puppetry producer and daily dubbing of ghosters, with the benediction of the Holy Genesius Archimimus and under the distinguished patronage of their Elderships the Oldens from the four coroners of Findrias, Murias, Gorias and Falias, Messoirs the Coarbs, Clive Sollis, Galorius Kettle, Pobiedo Lancey and Pierre Dusort, while the Caesar-in-Chief looks. On. Sennet. As played to the Adelphi by the Brothers Bratislavoff (Hyrcan and Haristobulus), after humpteen dumpteen revivals. Before all the King's Hoarsers with all the Queen's Mum. And wordloosed over seven seas crowdblast in cellleneteutoslavzendlatinsoundscript. In four tubbloids. While fern may cald us until firn make cold. *The Mime of Mick, Nick and the Maggies*, adopted from the Ballymooney Bloodriddon Murther by Bluechin Blackdillain. . . .

Time: the pressant.

With futurist onehorse balletbattle pictures and the Pageant of Past History worked up with animal variations amid everglaning mangrovemazes and beorbtracktors by Messrs Thud and Blunder. Shadows by the film folk, masses by the good people. Promptings by Elanio Vitale. Longshots, upcloses, outblacks and stagetolets by Hexenschuss, Coachmaher, Incubone and Rocknarrag. Creations tastefully designed by Madame Berthe Delamode. Dances arranged by Harley Quinn and Coollimbeina. Jests, jokes, jigs and jorums for the Wake lent from the properties of the late cemented Mr T. M. Finnegan R.I.C. Lipmasks and hairwigs by Ouida Nooikke. Limes and Floods by Crooker and Toll. Kopay pibe by Kappa Pedersen. Hoed Pine hat with twentyfour ventholes by Morgen. Bosse and stringbag from Heteroditheroe's and All Ladies' presents. Tree taken for grafted. Rock rent. Phenecian blends and Sourdanian doofpoosts by Shauvesourishe and Wohntbedarft. The oakmulberryeke with silktrick twomesh from Shop-Sowry, seedsmanchap. Grabstone beg from General Orders Mailed.

Finnegans Wake, pp. 219–21

Finnegans Wake has no basic concrete plot, for it is liable to vary from the cosmic to the domestic level in the twinkling of an eye. Late in the book there is a wholly domestic scene which has led some to believe that we finally hit on the 'real', all the rest being the dream of the man here described. But this too is a little play, and soon the kaleidoscope will shift again.

55

A cry off.

Where are we at all? and whenabouts in the name of space?

I don't understand. I fail to say. I dearsee you too.

House of the cedarbalm of mead. Garth of Fyon. Scene and property plot. Stagemanager's prompt. Interior of dwelling on outskirts of city. Groove two. Chamber scene. Boxed. Ordinary bedroom set. Salmonpapered walls. Back, empty Irish grate, Adam's mantel, with wilting elopement fan, soot and tinsel, condemned. North, wall with window practicable. Argentine in casement.

Vamp. Pelmit above. No curtains. Blind drawn. South, party wall. Bed for two with strawberry bedspread, wickerworker clubsessel and caneseated millikinstool. Bookshrine without, facetowel upon. Chair for one. Woman's garments on chair. Man's trousers with crossbelt braces, collar on bedknob. Man's corduroy surcoat with tabrets and taces, seapan nacre buttons on nail. Woman's gown on ditto. Over mantelpiece picture of Michael, lance, slaying Satan, dragon with smoke. Small table near bed, front. Bed with bedding. Spare. Flagpatch quilt. Yverdown design. Limes. Lighted lamp without globe, scarf, gazette, tumbler, quantity of water, julepot, ticker, side props, eventuals, man's gummy article, pink.

Finnegans Wake, pp. 558–9

The final gestures of Joyce's characters divide between the intransigence of Stephen Dedalus in the *Portrait* and *Ulysses* (see pp. 12 and 43), and the attempts at acceptance and reconciliation by Gabriel Conroy in 'The Dead' (p. 71), Bloom, and perhaps even Molly. *Finnegans Wake* closes on an even surer current, as Joyce once again gives the woman 'the last word'. The speaker here is the river that flows through Dublin, the Liffey, and she describes her own symbolic role.

56

Soft morning, city! Lsp! I am leafy speafing. Lpf! Folty and folty all the nights have falled on to long my hair. Not a sound, falling. Lispn! No wind no word. Only a leaf, just a leaf and then leaves. The woods are fond always. As were we their babes in. And robins in crews so. It is for me goolden wending. Unless? Away! Rise up, man of the hooths, you have slept so long! Or is it only so mesleems? On your pondered palm. Reclined from cape to pede. With pipe on bowl. Terce for a fiddler, sixt

for makmerriers, none for a Cole. Rise up now and aruse!
Norvena's over. I am leafy, your goolden, so you called
me, may me life, yea your goolden, silve me solve, exso-
gerraider! You did so drool. I was so sharm. But there's
a great poet in you too. Stout Stokes would take you offly.
So has he as bored me to slump. But am good and rested.
Taks to you, toddy, tan ye! Yawhawaw. Helpunto min,
helpas vin. Here is your shirt, the day one, come back.
The stock, your collar. Also your double brogues. A com-
forter as well. And here your iverol and everthelest your
umbr. And stand up tall! Straight. I want to see you
looking fine for me. With your brandnew big green belt
and all. Blooming in the very lotust and second to nill,
Budd! When you're in the buckly shuit Rosensharonals
near did for you. Fiftyseven and three, cosh, with the
bulge. Proudpurse Alby with his pooraroon Eireen, they'll.
Pride, comfytousness, enevy! You make me think of a
wonderdecker I once. Or somebalt thet sailder, the man
megallant, with the bangled ears. Or an earl was he, at
Lucan? Or, no, it's the Iren duke's I mean. Of somebrey
erse from the Dark Countries. Come and let us! We
always said we'd. And go abroad. Rathgreany way perhaps. The childher are still fast. There is no school today.
Them boys is so contrairy. The Head does be worrying
himself. Heel trouble and heal travel. Galliver and Gell-
over. Unless they changes by mistake. I seen the likes in
the twinngling of an aye. Som. So oft. Sim. Time after
time. The sehm asnuh. Two bredder as doffered as nors in
soun. When one of him sighs or one of him cries 'tis
you all over. No peace at all. . . . Anyway let her rain
for my time is come. I done me best when I was let.
Thinking always if I go all goes. A hundred cares, a
tithe of troubles and is there one who understands me?
One in a thousand of years of the nights? All me life
I have been lived among them but now they are becoming
lothed to me. And I am lothing their little warm tricks.
And lothing their mean cosy turns. And all the greedy

gushes out through their small souls. And all the lazy
leaks down over their brash bodies. How small it's all!
And me letting on to meself always. And lilting on all the
time. I thought you were all glittering with the noblest
of carriage. You're only a bumpkin. I thought you the
great in all things, in guilt and in glory. You're but a
puny. Home! My people were not their sort out beyond
there so far as I can. For all the bold and bad and bleary
they are blamed, the seahags. No! Nor for all our wild
dances in all their wild din. I can seen meself among them,
allaniuvia pulchrabelled. How she was handsome, the wild
Amazia, when she would seize to my other breast! And
what is she weird, haughty Niluna, that she will snatch
from my ownest hair! For 'tis they are the stormies. Ho
hang! Hang ho! And the clash of our cries till we spring
to be free. Auravoles, they says, never heed of your
name! But I'm loothing them that's here and all I lothe.
Loonely in me loneness. For all their faults. I am passing
out. O bitter ending! I'll slip away before they're up.
They'll never see. Nor know. Nor miss me. And it's old
and old it's sad and old it's sad and weary I go back to
you, my cold father, my cold mad father, my cold mad
feary father, till the near sight of the mere size of him,
the moyles and moyles of it, moananoaning, makes me
seasilt saltsick and I rush, my only, into your arms. I
see them rising! Save me from those therrble prongs!
Two more. Onetwo moremens more. So. Avelaval. My
leaves have drifted from me. All. But one clings still. I'll
bear it on me. To remind me of. Lff! So soft this morning,
ours. Yes. Carry me along, taddy, like you done through
the toyfair! If I seen him bearing down on me now
under whitespread wings like he'd come from Arkangels, I
sink I'd die down over his feet, humbly dumbly, only to
washup. Yes, tid. There's where. First. We pass through
grass behush the bush to. Whish! A gull. Gulls. Far calls.
Coming, far! End here. Us then. Finn, again! Take. Bus
softlhee, mememormee! Till thousendsthee. Lps. The keys

to. Given! A way a lone a last a loved a long the
                            Finnegans Wake, pp. 619–28

There is no fullstop, because the sentence continues—
on the very first page of the book. Like the symbol of the
snake with its tail in its mouth, signifying completeness,
circularity, eternity, or like the river which runs into the
sea, is absorbed into the clouds, rains on the land and
drains into the river, *Finnegans Wake* runs on forever.

Bibliography

A *Reference list of Joyce's works*

Chamber Music (1907) ed. William York Tindall, Columbia University Press, New York, 1954.

The Critical Writings of James Joyce, ed. Ellsworth Mason and Richard Ellmann, Oxford University Press, London and New York, 1959.

Dubliners (1914) Jonathan Cape, 1967, and Penguin Books, 1965, Lodon; Compass Books (The Viking Press), New York, 1958.

The Essential James Joyce, ed. Harry Levin, Jonathan Cape, London, 1948; Penguin Books, London, 1963. Contains complete texts of A *Portrait of the Artist, Collected Poems, Exiles and Dubliners*.

Exiles (1918) Jonathan Cape, London, 1952; The Viking Press, New York, 1951.

Finnegans Wake (1939) Faber & Faber, London, 1964; The Viking Press, New York, 1964.

James Joyce's Scribbledehobble, ed. Thomas E. Connolly, Northwestern University Press, Evanston, Ill., 1961.

Letters of James Joyce, Vol. I, ed. Stuart Gilbert, Faber & Faber, London, and The Viking Press, New York, 1957;

Vols. II and III, ed. Richard Ellmann, Faber & Faber, London, and The Viking Press, New York, 1966.

The Portable James Joyce, ed. Harry Levin, The Viking Press, New York, 1947.

A Portrait of the Artist as a Young Man (1916) Jonathan Cape, 1956, and Penguin Books, 1960, London; Compass Books (The Viking Press) New York, 1964.

Stephen Hero (1944) ed. Theodore Spencer, Jonathan Cape, London, 1956; New Directions, New York, 1955.

Ulysses (1922) The Bodley Head, London, 1960; The Modern Library, New York, 1961.

The Workshop of Daedalus, ed. Robert Scholes and Richard M. Kain, Northwestern University Press, Evanston, Ill., 1965. Contains *Epiphanies*.

B *Bibliographies*

DEMING, ROBERT H., *A Biliography of James Joyce Studies*, University of Kansas Libraries, 1964. Includes studies of separate works to December 1961.

The James Joyce Quarterly, ed. Thomas P. Staley, University of Tulsa, Oklahoma. First issue, Fall 1963. Besides articles on Joyce, publishes a yearly Joyce bibliography.

SLOCUM, JOHN J. and CAHOON, HERBERT, *A Bibliography of James Joyce*, Yale University Press, London and New Haven, Conn., 1953. Editions, translations, manuscripts, musical settings of Joyce's own works to 1950.

C *Biographical works*

BEACH, SYLVIA, *Shakespeare and Company*, New York, 1959. Memoirs of the American bookseller who published *Ulysses* from her shop in Paris.

COLUM, MARY and PADRAIC. *Our Friend James Joyce*, Doubleday & Co., New York, 1958. The authors, Irish artists in their own right, comment on their university days and other meetings with Joyce.

ELLMANN, RICHARD, *James Joyce*. Oxford University Press, London and New York, 1959. The standard biography.

HEALEY, GEORGE HARRIS, ed. *The Dublin Diary of Stanislaus Joyce*. Faber & Faber, London, and Cornell University Press, Ithaca, N.Y., 1962. A diary kept in 1903-4 by Joyce's precocious younger brother.

JOYCE, STANISLAUS, *My Brother's Keeper*, Faber & Faber, London, and The Viking Press, New York, 1958. A memoir of the relationship between the Joyce brothers.

D   Critical works

ADAMS, ROBERT MARTIN, *Surface and Symbol, The Consistency of James Joyce's 'Ulysses'*, Oxford University Press, New York, 1962. The 'factual' basis of *Ulysses* and comments on its relation to 'symbols' sometimes mistaken.

ATHERTON, JAMES S., *The Books at the Wake, A Study of Literary Allusions in James Joyce's 'Finnegans Wake'*, Faber & Faber, London, and The Viking Press, New York, 1960. With an alphabetical list of literary allusions.

BLAMIRES, HARRY. *The Bloomsday Book*, Methuen & Co., London, 1966. A condensed straightforward paraphrase of *Ulysses*. Useful for beginners.

BUDGEN, FRANK, *James Joyce and the Making of Ulysses*, Grayson, London 1934; Indiana University Press, Bloomington, Ind., 1960 Part 'guide', part memoirs of the English artist's friendship with Joyce in Zurich.

CAMPBELL, JOSEPH and ROBINSON, HENRY MORTON, *A Skeleton Key to Finnegans Wake*, Faber & Faber, London, and Harcourt Brace, New York, 1944.

BIBLIOGRAPHY

CONNOLLY, THOMAS E., ed., *Joyce's Portrait, Criticisms and Critiques*, Peter Owen, London, 1964; Appleton-Century-Crofts, New York, 1962. Reprinted articles by scholars.

GILBERT, STUART, *James Joyce's 'Ulysses'*, second edition, revised: Faber & Faber, London, 1952; Vintage Books, New York, 1955. An early guide by a French scholar who knew Joyce in Paris. Good on Homeric and esoteric symbolism.

GIVENS, SEON, ed., *James Joyce: Two Decades of Criticism* Vanguard Press, New York, 1948. Essays by prominent scholars and writers.

GLASHEEN, ADLINE, *A Census of Finnegans Wake*, Faber & Faber, London, 1957; Northwestern University Press, Evanston, Ill., 1956; *A Second Census*, Northwestern University Press, 1963. Alphabetical listing of all characters, fictional and factual.

GOLDBERG, S. L., *The Classical Temper, A Study of James Joyce's 'Ulysses'*, Chatto and Windus, London, and Barnes and Noble, New York, 1961.

GOLDBERG, S. L., *Joyce*, Oliver & Boyd, Edinburgh and London, 1962; Grove Press, New York, 1963. Short introductory survey, weak on *Finnegans Wake*.

GOLDMAN, ARNOLD, *The Joyce Paradox*, Routledge and Kegan Paul, London, and Northwestern University Press, Evanston, Ill., 1966. The development of structure in Joyce.

HANLEY, MILES L., *Word Index to James Joyce's 'Ulysses'*, University of Wisconsin Press, Madison, Wisc., 1953. Pagination and lineation to the pre-1961 Random House/Modern Library text.

HART, CLIVE, *Concordance to Finnegans Wake*, University of Minisota, Minneapolis, Minn., 1963. Even parts of words are listed, with page and line references.

HART, CLIVE, *Structure and Motif in Finnegans Wake*,
106

Faber & Faber, London, and Northwestern University Press, Evanston, Ill., 1962. Not a complete exposition of the novel's structure, but excellent on the portions it describes.

HODGART, MATTHEW and WORTHINGTON, MABEL P., *Song in the Work of James Joyce*, Columbia University Press, New York, 1959. Including an alphabetical listing of songs mentioned in Joyce.

KAIN, RICHARD M., *Fabulous Voyager*, University of Chicago, Chicago, Ill., 1947, and Compass Books (The Viking Press), New York, 1949. Guide to *Ulysses* with indices of motifs, characteristics of Bloom, *etc.*

KENNER, HUGH, *Dublin's Joyce*, Chatto & Windus, London, 1955; Indiana University Press, Bloomington Ind. 1956. Spirited, inventive, ultimately ambivalent and undersophisticated, about symbolism.

LEVIN, HARRY, *James Joyce: A Critical Introduction*, New Directions, Norfolk, Conn., 1941; revised edn. Faber & Faber, London, and New Directions, New York, 1960. Best introduction.

LITZ, A. WALTON, *The Art of James Joyce*, Oxford University Press, London and New York, 1961. Joyce's literary methods and revisions in his later work.

MAGALANER, MARVIN, *Time of Apprenticeship: The Fiction of Young James Joyce*, Abelard-Schumann, London and New York, 1959. Mainly on *Dubliners*.

MAGALANER, MARVIN, ed., *A James Joyce Miscellany*, New York University Press, New York, 1957; *A James Joyce Miscellany: Second Series*, Southern Illinois University Press, Carbondale, Ill., 1959; *A James Joyce Miscellany: Third Series*, Southern Illinois University Press, Carbondale, Ill., 1962. Essays by critics and scholars.

MAGALANER, MARVIN and KAIN, RICHARD M., *Joyce: the Man, the Work, the Reputation*, New York University

Press, New York, 1956; John Calder, London, 1965.

MORRIS, W. E. and NAULT, C. A. Jnr., eds., *Portraits of an Artist: a Casebook on James Joyce's 'A Portrait'*, Odyssey Press, New York, 1962.

MORSE, J. MITCHELL, *The Sympathetic Alien*, New York University Press, New York, 1959. Joyce and Catholic themes.

NOON, WILLIAM T., *Joyce and Aquinas*, Yale University Press, London and New Haven, Conn., 1957. Particularly valuable on theoretical aesthetic elements.

PRESCOTT, JOSEPH, *Exploring James Joyce*, Southern Illinois University Press, Carbondale, Ill., 1964. Good on the various manuscript stages of *Ulysses*, and on how Joyce built up his characterisation of Bloom and Molly.

RYF, ROBERT S., *A New Approach to Joyce*, University of California Press, Berkeley and Los Angeles, 1962. Uses *A Portrait* to explore Joyce's other fiction, oversimplifies symbolism.

SCHUTTE, WILLIAM, *Joyce and Shakespeare*, Yale University Press, London and New Haven, Conn., 1957. Includes tabulation of allusions to Shakespeare.

SULLIVAN, KEVIN, *Joyce Among the Jesuits*, Columbia University Press, New York, 1958.

SULTAN, STANLEY, *The Argument of 'Ulysses'*, Ohio State University Press, Columbus, Ohio, 1965. Chapter-by-chapter analysis.

TINDALL, WILLIAM Y., *James Joyce, His Way of Interpreting the Modern World*. Scribner's, New York, 1950. Best on *Finnegans Wake*.

TINDALL, WILLIAM Y., *A Readers Guide to James Joyce*, Thames and Hudson, London, and Noonday Press, New York, 1959.